β+T
6 May 01

W9-BXT-250

George Washington
CITIZEN-SOLDIER

George Washington
CITIZEN-SOLDIER

Charles Cecil Wall

University Press of Virginia

CHARLOTTESVILLE

Wingate College Library

THE UNIVERSITY PRESS OF VIRGINIA
Copyright © 1980 by the Rector and Visitors
of the University of Virginia

First published 1980

Library of Congress Cataloging in Publication Data
Wall, Charles Cecil.
George Washington, citizen-soldier.
Bibliography: p.
Includes index.
1. Washington, George, Pres. U.S., 1732–1799.
2. Presidents—United States—Biography.
I. Title.
E312.W29   973.3'092'4 [B]   79-21241
ISBN 0-8139-0851-5
ISBN 0-8139-0852-3 pbk.

Printed in the United States of America

GEORGE WASHINGTON BY PEALE

In May of 1772 George Washington posed for his first portrait. On this important occasion he chose to appear in the uniform that he had worn as colonel of the Virginia Regiment. A passage in his letter to Jonathan Boucher, the tutor of his stepson, indicates that he was an unwilling and uncooperative subject. He confided to Boucher that he sat for Peale "in so grave, so sullen a mood, and now and then under the influence of Morpheus when some critical strokes are making that I fancy the skill of the gentleman's pencil will be put to it in describing to the world what manner of man I am." The uniform portrayed in this portrait is probably the one he wore while attending the Second Continental Congress in Philadelphia. This portrait hung in the Mount Vernon west parlor until 1802, when it was inherited by Mrs. Washington's grandson, George Washington Parke Custis.
(From the Collection of Washington and Lee University, Lexington, Virginia.)

082062

I never knew but one man who resolved not to forget the citizen in the soldier or ruler and that was G.W. and I am afraid I shall not know another.

Landon Carter's Diary
3 May 1776

Contents

List of Illustrations

Preface

Every schoolboy knows that Henry Lee eulogized his neighbor, companion-in-arms, and intimate friend George Washington as "First in War, first in peace and first in the hearts of his countrymen." But very few know that Lee completed this sentence with the words, "he was second to none in the humble and endearing scenes of private life."

Mount Vernon, of course, was the setting for those scenes. Washington's preference for the domestic life and the rural pursuits that centered there is attested in his writings: "I can truly say I had rather be at Mount Vernon with a friend or two about me, than to be attended at the seat of government by the officers of state and the representatives of every power in Europe." While it may be difficult for the present-day student to take this statement seriously, it was sincere. It is basically revealing; and it must be accepted if George Washington is to be understood in the roles he played.

For Washington, the larger world was a stage. No figures of speech recur more frequently in his writings than those which refer to his public activities in theatrical terms. At the seat of government, at headquarters, on the field of battle, he saw himself as an actor. His role, played with dignity and sincerity, was great drama, but it was theatre, and as Lee was aware, the biographer can discover the full measure of the man only in the scenes of private life and in his personal correspondence—his letters to his managers, his family, and his intimate friends.

During the Revolutionary War letters were exchanged with almost weekly regularity between General Washington and his Mount Vernon manager and cousin, Lund Washington. When Mrs. Washington was at home, there were frequent letters to her. The general also corresponded less frequently with his stepson, John Parke Custis, who much of the time was in residence with his young family at Mount Vernon. As in all his correspondence with family and intimate friends, these letters were more confiding and more revealing of his personality in the freedom of expression he allowed himself than were his reports to his official correspondents. In the aggregate they would have constituted a history of the Revolution, in weekly installments, by its principal participant. The pity is that only a minor portion of them survived. The destruction of his correspondence with Mrs. Washington, by her own hand a short time before her death, was almost total; only two letters escaped this literary and historical disaster. The destruction of Lund Washington's correspondence with his employer, at Lund's deathbed request, was less than complete: by an unexplained happenstance, over forty of Lund's letters to the general survived. Of the general's letters to Lund, thirty-two are extant, half of them in the form of copies (some but partial) which were retained at headquarters. Twenty-two of his letters to his stepson survive.

There is some compensation for these losses in other sources. Lund's domestic ledger is a mine of information and a local record of the wartime inflation. The general's letters to other members of the family and to a few intimates among his fellow Virginians carry much the same news, in the same personal vein, as did the now-missing letters to Mrs. Washington and to Lund at Mount Vernon. The journals and letters of those who enjoyed the hospitality of Mount Vernon in the course of their wartime travels also contribute to the record. From these varied sources there emerges a portrait of George Washington as a citizen-soldier, a general who in the midst of his military preoccupations finds welcome diversion in writing detailed directions for the planting of groves and shrubberies about his distant dwelling on the bank of the Potomac or the drawing of plans for a new Mount Vernon stable. In their range of content these selections present a composite portrait of the man identified in the full text of Lee's eulogistic sentence. Here he appears as soldier, statesman, husband, husbandman, and neighbor, in constant perspective and at human, rather than monumental, scale.

One of the nation's greatest physical heritages from that period is, of course, Mount Vernon itself, the setting for those endearing scenes of private life which were remarked upon by Lee. It survives as a landmark of the Revolution, for it was during those years that most of the present structures were developed under Lund Washington's supervision. It reminds us of Mrs. Washington's departure each autumn or early winter to join the general at his quarters and her homecoming in the spring or early summer to an anxious period of waiting and hoping.

During the Revolution this isolated domestic enclave became a symbol of its master's faith in a destiny that would bring victory to the forces he commanded and in a benign Providence that would allow him a period of retirement "under his own vine and fig tree." In the present age Mount Vernon's beauty, order, and dignity evoke an image of its architect, at the same time reminding us of his determination to inhabit the home of his choice in dignity and freedom.

My grateful acknowledgments are due to the Mount Vernon Ladies' Association for making available the resources of its reference library, which is so rich in unpublished material relating to the Washington and Custis families and to the life at Mount Vernon during the last half of the eighteenth century in all of its diversity. As citations have been omitted in the text it is noted here that these materials are properly catalogued and indexed and that they are available to the serious student by appointment. I acknowledge with appreciation, also, the privilege of drawing upon the association's collection of portraits and other memorabilia for illustrations which lend an added dimension to this volume.

To my former staff associates, John Castellani, Christine

Meadows, Mildred Payne, and Ellen McCallister, I am indebted for constant, effective cooperation. Their professional skills and intimate knowledge of the collection were of invaluable assistance.

My abundant thanks are extended to Washington and Lee University for permission to reproduce five of the family portraits which Martha Washington bequeathed to her grandson, George Washington Parke Custis, and which passed from his grandson, General Custis Lee, to the university. The Colonial Williamsburg Foundation has generously allowed me to quote from the journals of Nicholas Cresswell and Philip Vickers Fithian and from Rutherfoord Goodwin's *Brief and True Report Concerning Williamsburg in Virginia*. I am also indebted to the foundation for permission to use two illustrations from its facsimile publication of the *Journal of Major George Washington*, 1754. Grateful acknowledgement is due also to Helen Hill Miller, to Parke Rouse, and to C. Waller Barrett for constructive criticism and knowledgeable counseling.

The brief bibliography that follows the text is restricted to works that contributed directly to my study. My indebtedness to those preeminent authorities on George Washington, John C. Fitzpatrick and Douglas Southall Freeman, deserves to be emphasized.

PART I

The Making of a Rebel

I never deny, or even hesitate in granting any request that is made to me (especially by persons I esteem, and in matters of moment) without a feeling of in expressable uneasiness.

George Washington to a neighbor, January 1775

The Making of a Rebel

THE EARLY YEARS

If we would understand George Washington in his role as citizen-soldier and principal founding father, we should look first to the earlier years of his life, with particular attention to the circumstances and the incidents that transformed him from a loyal subject of His Majesty George the Third into a belligerent rebel. Of his early childhood little is known, probably because it was not much different from the lives of his youthful contemporaries whose families were comfortably established on other tidewater Virginia plantations. The family Bible at Mount Vernon records his birth on the twenty-second (Old Style eleventh) of February 1732. He was the eldest of the five children of Augustine Washington by his second wife, Mary Ball. When George was three years old, his father moved his young family from the birthplace at Bridges Creek on the lower Potomac to his Hunting Creek plantation (later known as Mount Vernon) on the same river, a few miles below Alexandria. Three years later Augustine moved again, this time to Ferry Farm on the Rappahannock River, just below the little town of Fredericksburg. There Augustine died of "gout of the stomach" in April 1743. His Potomac River properties were bequeathed to Lawrence and Augustine, Jr., older sons by his first marriage. His four sons by his second marriage were each assured a modest inheritance of land and slaves on reaching the age of twenty-one.

3

In May 1747 a letter to Mary Ball Washington from her elder half brother, Joseph Ball, in London reveals that a nautical career was being considered for her fifteen-year-old son. Joseph Ball, a man of affairs and well qualified to counsel the young mother, wrote:

I understand you are advised and have some thought of sending your son George to sea. I think he had better be put apprentice to a tinker; for a common sailor before the mast has by no means the common liberty of the Subject; for they will press him from a ship where he has 50 shillings a month and make him take three and twenty; and cut him and staple him and use him like a Negro, or rather, like a dog. And as for any considerable preferment in the Navy, it is not to be expected, there are always too many grasping for it here, who have interest, and he has none. And if he should get to be master of a Virginia ship (which would be very difficult to do) a planter that has three or four hundred acres of land and three or four slaves, if he be industrious, may live more comfortably, and leave his family in better Bread, than such a master of a ship can.

Young George did not go to sea, of course, a decision for which his Uncle Joseph may deserve credit. Of the youth's own sentiments on the subject of a maritime career, of disappointment or resentment of discrimination that might handicap him as a young colonial seeking a career, there is no record. Memoranda in his own handwriting indicate that he may have already commenced running lines with a tripod and surveying instruments that had belonged to his father. These notes reveal that during the summer of 1747 he surveyed tracts for some of his Washington cousins who lived along the Potomac east of Fredericksburg. In February 1748 he surveyed his half brother Lawrence's turnip field at Mount Vernon. In the spring of 1748 with Lawrence's brother-in-law, George William Fairfax, he joined a surveying party that had been engaged to run the lines of tracts in the westernmost portion of Lord Fairfax's Northern Neck Proprietary, a five-million-acre domain extending from Chesapeake Bay westward between the Potomac and Rappahannock rivers to a western boundary that had just been established between the

4

headwaters of those rivers. This venture into the wilderness beyond the Blue Ridge marked the end of George Washington's boyhood and determined his first adult role. On 20 July 1749, at the age of seventeen, he was certified as the official surveyor of Culpepper County, qualified to survey anywhere in Virginia. Soon he was on a surveying mission in the Shenandoah Valley under the auspices of Col. William Fairfax, father-in-law of his brother Lawrence.

THE YOUNG SURVEYOR

Belvoir, the seat of Col. William Fairfax, was situated on a commanding bluff overlooking the Potomac just below Mount Vernon. William was a first cousin of Thomas, Lord Fairfax, and His Lordship's agent for the Fairfax Proprietary—responsible for granting lands, enforcing the terms of the grants, and collecting the annual quitrents. His earlier careers had included brief service in the British army before crossing the Atlantic to assume a civilian post in the Bahamas. For a period before coming to Virginia he was a collector of customs in New England. Since entering the service of his cousin in 1734 he had become collector of customs for the lower Potomac, a justice of Fairfax County, and a member of the Governor's Council. By virtue of his abilities, his broad background, and the positions he held, William Fairfax was the most influential man in Northern Virginia. George William Fairfax, the oldest son of Colonel William, had been born in the Bahamas and educated in England. He was four years younger than his brother-in-law Lawrence Washington and seven years older than Lawrence's half brother George. He was a member of the county court and of the House of Burgesses. In December 1748 George William married Sarah Cary—Sally to her friends—daughter of Col. Wilson Cary of Ceelys on the James River near Hampton, and brought his young bride to Belvoir. The ties between Belvoir and Mount Vernon were close, and it was the good fortune of Lawrence's young half brother to be accepted as a member of the family and included in the joint activities of the two households.

In the autumn of 1751 young Washington's career as a surveyor was interrupted by a voyage to Barbados with his ailing brother Lawrence, who was stricken with consumption and hoped to benefit by a change of climate. There is a journal account of this journey, but the document is badly mutilated. Two weeks after they landed at Bridgetown, the journalist notes (17 November) that he "was strongly attacked by the small-pox; sent for Dr. Lanahan whose attendance was very constant 'till my recovery, and going out, which was not 'till Thursday the twelfth of December." George Washington carried the facial blemishes of this disease to his grave, but he had gained lifelong immunity.

As Lawrence's health did not improve, it was arranged that he would go on to Bermuda in search of a better environment and his companion would return to Virginia. George sailed on 22 December. His vessel came safely to anchor in the York River on 26 or 27 January 1752. There were letters to be delivered to Governor Dinwiddie, who received him graciously, inquired about the health of his brother, and kept him to dinner. From Williamsburg he made his way to Mount Vernon by 5 or 6 February with a report to his sister-in-law on the condition of her husband. His business ledger establishes that he was soon back at work with his surveying equipment in the Shenandoah Valley.

In June Lawrence Washington returned home from Bermuda; the time had come to put his affairs in order. He died on 26 July 1752, leaving a complicated and vaguely drawn will. His widow was to have a life interest in Mount Vernon, which would then pass to their only daughter, Sarah. If Sarah died without issue, the property was to pass to his half brother George.

Of more immediate moment was the successorship to Lawrence's position as Adjutant General of the Colony, which by prearrangement was to be divided among three men, each of whom would have a district. George was a candidate for one of these districts, no doubt with the encouragement and ad-

LAWRENCE WASHINGTON (1718–52)

Fig. 1. Lawrence Washinton was the elder half brother of George.
(Courtesy of the Mount Vernon Ladies' Association.)

vocacy of William Fairfax. In November he was allotted the southern district of Virginia. A year later he would be reassigned to the adjutancy of the Northern Neck and the Eastern Shore. The position carried the title of major; the annual salary was £100. The routine duties were mustering militia units, witnessing drills, and inspecting equipment. He would put aside his chain and sextant, exchange the drab garb of a surveyor for a military uniform, and strap on a sword. For a twenty-year-old Virginian who yearned to excel, it must have been an exciting transition!

A WINTER JOURNEY

At mid-century a state of peace existed between France and England, but this was merely a truce established by the Treaty of Aix-la-Chapelle in 1748. The two nations were engaged in a contest for world empire, and both claimed the Ohio Valley, each believing that the possession of this territory was vital to its security. When Governor Dinwiddie reported French encroachments on the Virginia frontier to the home government in the summer of 1753, he was instructed to warn the intruders, and if they refused to withdraw, he was to drive them out. In November Dinwiddie reported that he had sent an adjutant of the militia with an admonitory letter to the French commandant on the Ohio. His emissary was George Washington, a choice that had been approved by the Governor's Council. The record indicates that the young adjutant had volunteered his services. It seems highly probable that he did so on the basis of information and encouragement from his friend and mentor Col. William Fairfax.

With his commission Washington received a formal passport and a letter of instructions. On his arrival in the Ohio country he was to seek out the Half King and other well-disposed chieftains of the Six Nations, to announce his mission, and to enlist their assistance. He was to be diligent in collecting information as to the location and construction of French forts, the numbers and disposition of their forces, and all evidence of their intentions. His letter delivered and reply in hand, he was to take his leave and "return immediately back." If rumors were true, the situation demanded prompt countermeasures: the next summer might be critical. It seems remarkable that such a delicate and important mission would have been entrusted to a youth of twenty-one!

In Fredericksburg Washington engaged a young Dutchman who spoke French, Jacob Van Braam, to accompany him in the role of interpreter. At Wills Creek (now Cumberland, Maryland), Christopher Gist honored the governor's request that he act as guide. Gist, a man in his forties, had traveled widely as a surveyor and explorer on the frontiers of North Carolina and Virginia. He was a person of zeal and integrity, well-versed in the ways and wiles of the Indians. Four servitors completed the party.

The envoy extraordinary and his equestrian escort set out from Wills Creek on 15 November and reached Logstown, headquarters of the Half King, a few miles below the Forks of the Ohio (now Pittsburgh) on the twenty-fifth. En route they had encountered excessive rains and a "Vast quantity of Snow." Here five days were consumed in bringing together the chief men among the local Indians, explaining their mission, exchanging belts of wampum with appropriate protocol, and enlisting support. The Half King and four others accompanied the party to their next destination, Venango, an old Indian town about seventy miles to the north, where there was a French post. Here they learned that the French commandant was at Fort Le Boeuf, just below Lake Erie, so they pressed on. At Le Boeuf, as at Venango, the French were polite and hospitable, but at both places they tried to inebriate and detach the Half King and his fellows.

The commandant's response to Governor Dinwiddie's letter curtly dismissed "the pretensions of the King of Great Britain." Most of the French troops had been withdrawn northward for the winter, but there were over two hundred canoes at the fort and more in the making. They were obviously intended to carry an expedition southward in the spring or early summer.

On 15 December Washington left Fort Le Boeuf, intent on making speedy delivery of the commandant's letter. At Venango, when the Half King and his companions paused for liquid refreshment, he impatiently left them behind. South of Venango, as his horses weakened and faltered, he detailed Van Braam and the hostlers to bring them on and forged ahead with Gist, in Indian garb, carrying only their packs and rifles. Along the way they disarmed and evaded an Indian who volunteered his services as guide, then treacherously tried to shoot them down at close range but missed his mark. Gist wanted to kill the man but was overruled by his companion. As they crossed the Allegheny River on a primitive raft of their own construction, Washington had a narrow escape from drowning when he tumbled into deep water while trying to dislodge their craft from an ice floe. East of the river there was a brief delay in procuring horses, but on 7 January 1754 Washington notes their arrival at Wills Creek, "after as fatiguing a journey as it is possible to conceive." On the eleventh he reached Belvoir and there tarried for a day of rest and recuperation. On the sixteenth he delivered the French commandant's letter to the governor in Williamsburg. He also submitted a map of the country he had traversed west of the Alleghenies, a plan of Fort Le Boeuf, and a report based on his journal. The closing sentence of the latter expressed the hope that "it will be sufficient to satisfy your Honor with my Proceedings: for that was my Aim in undertaking the Journey & chief study throughout the Prosecution of it." The report was presented to the Governor's Council and published in the Virginia *Gazette*. Copies were sent to his Majesty's secretary for the Colonies. It was reprinted in several colonial papers and in London. The House of Burgesses

THE JOURNAL OF MAJOR WASHINGTON

Fig. 2. Facsimile of the title page of Washington's journal. *(Courtesy of The Colonial Williamsburg Foundation.)*

THE
JOURNAL
OF

Major *George Washington,*

SENT BY THE

Hon. *ROBERT DINWIDDIE,* Esq;
His Majesty's Lieutenant-Governor, and
Commander in Chief of *VIRGINIA,*

TO THE

COMMANDANT

· OF THE

FRENCH FORCES

ON

O H I O.

TO WHICH ARE ADDED, THE

GOVERNOR's LETTER,

AND A TRANSLATION OF THE

FRENCH OFFICER's ANSWER.

WILLIAMSBURG:

Printed by WILLIAM HUNTER. 1754.

11

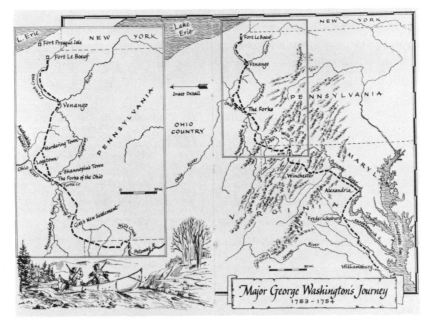

MAP OF MAJOR WASHINGTON'S JOURNEY

Fig. 3. Map of Washington's journey from Williamsburg to Fort Le Boeuf
and return.
(Courtesy of The Colonial Williamsburg Foundation.)

voted the sum of £50 to GEORGE WASHINGTON "to testify our
Approbation of his Proceedings on his Journey to the Ohio."
Certainly this winter journey of more than a thousand miles
had been a remarkable demonstration of courage, intelligence,
and physical stamina—a combination of qualities that should
be in demand.

FORT NECESSITY AND BRADDOCK'S DEFEAT

His next assignment was not long in materializing. It found
him on a morning in early April 1754 at the head of the first
detachment of the Virginia Regiment en route from Alexan-

12

dria to the forks of the Ohio by way of Winchester and Wills Creek. He was now, at the age of twenty-two, Lieutenant-Colonel Washington, second in regimental command to Col. Joshua Fry—who was to complete the recruiting of the regiment and to follow the first unit in a supporting capacity. They were to complete a fort then under construction by a small force at the forks and to defend the king's domain against the encroachments of the French. The valiant mood of the young lieutenant-colonel found expression in his letter to Governor Sharpe of Maryland urging his support of the expedition. The cause, he wrote, was one that should rouse the heroic spirit of every freeborn Englishman to attest the rights and privileges of the king and to "rescue from the invasions of a usurping enemy, our Majesty's property, his dignity and land."

Near Wills Creek the westbound column encountered Ensign Ward, the officer who had been in charge of the work force at the Forks. He and his men had been run off by a large French force, which had come down the river in a flotilla of three hundred canoes and supporting bateaux. The French were now busily carrying on the work they had interrupted.

At a council of war it was decided that the detachment would continue westward, opening a road for the troops that were to follow with wheeled transport and artillery. Ward was sent on to Williamsburg with a plea that reinforcements, munitions, and provisions be sent with all possible speed. It was a brave decision, necessary if the Indian allies were to be supported and retained; their defection to the enemy could be disastrous.

In late May Washington was warned by the Half King that a small French scouting party was lurking in the vicinity of his encampment at Great Meadows. With the cooperation of the Half King and his companions, Washington and his men took the hostile party by surprise in its place of concealment. Ten were killed in a brief exchange of fire or, if they had been wounded, were knocked in the head by the Indians and, as Washington expressed it in his report to Governor Dinwid-

Wingate College Library

die, "bereiv'd of their scalps." Among the dead was the leader of the party, the sieur de Jumonville. Twenty-two prisoners were taken and marched off to Winchester. The Virginia regiment lost only one man.

Shortly after this encounter, word came that Colonel Fry had died of an injury sustained in a fall from his horse. Soon after, Washington received his commission as full colonel and commandant of the regiment. Work went forward on the road, but there was a continuing shortage of transport, a threat of starvation, and a scarcity of ammunition. Late in June a trustworthy Indian sent word of an impending attack by a greatly superior force of French and Indians. The Virginians were hastily concentrated at Great Meadows; the stockade there was strengthened and christened Fort Necessity. The Indian allies, sensing disaster, silently faded away. The total effective force, including a company of British regulars under command of a Captain Mackay, numbered less than three hundred. The attack came on the morning of 3 July. In the course of the day the besieged garrison suffered one hundred casualties in killed and wounded. All of their horses and cattle were killed, and with the loss of the latter they were reduced to three days rations. Their entrenchments had been flooded by a heavy downpour; their powder was damp. As darkness came on, the soldiers broke into the rum and were rapidly becoming undependable. At this unhappy moment the French issued an invitation to parley. Van Braam was sent out and returned with terms that were refused; they would not surrender their arms! This amendment was accepted, and in due course Van Braam returned with a rain-blotted document in French that, in his verbal translation, offered honorable terms. The leader of the French force, a brother of Jumonville and the author of the paper, premised that no state of war existed; they had come only to avenge the killing of his brother. Two hostages would be detained to assure the return of the Frenchmen who were being held prisoner. The remainder of the garrison would be free to march out with their arms and their regimental colors. These conditions were accepted.

The potentialities of this occasion had not been lost on the relatively untried commandant of the regiment. Although himself a conspicuous target, he had come through the day unscathed. He had confirmed his assurance to Governor Dinwiddie that he had "a constitution hardy enough to encounter and undergo the most severe trials, . . . and resolution to face what any man durst." He might well have been singled out as a hostage, but Van Braam and another junior officer had been accepted in that role. Memory of the day never dimmed. Twenty-two years later, in July 1776 on Manhattan Island at another moment of great menace, he noted in a letter to Gen. Adam Stephen, who had been with him at Fort Necessity as a young lieutenant, "I did not let the third pass off without a grateful remembrance of the escape we had. . . . The same Providence that protected us . . . will, I hope continue his mercies."

Not until later was the true import of the articles of capitulation discovered. Thanks to the ineptitude or deliberate evasion of Van Braam, Washington and Captain Mackay had signed an acknowledgment of responsibility for "l'assassinat" of Jumonville, "porteur d'une sommation" — literally, the assassination of the bearer of a message. Van Braam had translated *l'assassinat* as the "death", "killing," or "loss." It was distressing; there was indignation and denunciation of Van Braam.

In Williamsburg and elsewhere throughout the colonies, no criticism was directed at Washington for the surrender and the retreat to Wills Creek that followed. The Virginia *Gazette* reflected the prevailing opinion that a few brave men had been exposed and sacrificed by the negligence "of those who, in obedience to their Sovereign's command ought to have been with them many months before." Privately, both in Williamsburg and in London, it might have been conceded that the attack on Jumonville had been a bit impetuous, but the French concept of Jumonville as a peaceful emissary was rejected. At the Virginia capitol in October Washington had the satisfaction of acknowledging on behalf of himself and his fellow officers the formal thanks of the House of Burgesses "for our behavior in the late unsuccessful engagement with the French." He expressed the hope that their future services would entitle them to a continuance of that body's approbation. In England it was conceded that Washington and his men had displayed courage and resolution, but their military competence was doubted. The earl of Albemarle, titular governor of Virginia in absentia and Ambassador to France, wrote "Officers, and good ones, must be sent to discipline the militia and to lead them. . . . " Albemarle may have been reading the reports of his Virginia deputy, who for some time had been urging that two regiments be sent from England to spearhead an expedition which would regain the valley of the Ohio.

Dinwiddie, a dour and thrifty Scotsman, had also been doing his best to discourage and suppress the appeals of Washington and his fellow officers for parity with those of corresponding rank in the British military establishment. In March, when Washington discovered that his own pay was to be even less than Dinwiddie had promised, he had been so indignant that he was dissuaded from renouncing his commission only by William Fairfax's assurance that he would endeavor to have more money allocated to the officers. Parity with the regulars was not suggested, but Dinwiddie had issued a proclamation setting aside 200,000 acres on the Ohio as a bounty for the members of the Virginia regiment.

In mid-May, as the officers of the regiment faced the prospect of serving alongside a company of regulars, they had drafted a formal protest of the discriminations under which they labored and tendered it to Washington for transmittal to the governor. In his covering letter, the colonel expressed sympathy with the protest. For his own part, he wrote, he would really prefer to serve without pay than accede to such "ignoble" terms. The governor thought the protest ill-founded and was annoyed by Washington's endorsement of it. Finally, on 10 June, Washington attempted to end an interchange that seemed to serve no purpose. He wrote "For the last time I must say that this will be a cancer that will grate some officers of this Regiment beyond all measure to serve upon such different terms when their lives, their fortunes and their characters are equally and I dare say as effectually exposed as those who are happy enough to have King's Commissions." A few days later he could not refrain from adding a postscript on the subject. The cancer was eating at him also, aggravated by the fact that a captain with a king's commission outranked a Virginia colonel. "The rank of officers," he wrote, "is much dearer than the pay."

In Williamsburg, having made his acknowledgments to the House of Burgesses in the expectation of continuing in the service, Washington learned that the forces of North Carolina, Virginia, and Maryland would be united under the command of Governor Sharpe of Maryland, who had just received a royal commission as lieutenant-colonel. The Virginia regiment was to be broken into independent companies; he faced a three-grade demotion to a captaincy of one of these companies! He tendered his resignation to Governor Dinwiddie, and it was accepted without protest. Governor Sharpe, through an aide, urged him to remain in the service, but he rode off toward Fredericksburg and Fairfax County without committing himself. At Belvoir, with Col. William Fairfax, George William, and Sally, he found the spiritual therapy and the advice he sought. From Belvoir on 15 November 1754, he wrote to Sharpe's aide declining the governor's offer. He expressed his appreciation of their consideration and his regret at leaving the service. With the advice and concurrence of his friends, he was doing so, he wrote, "to obey the call of honor." He then added in closing, "My inclinations are strongly bent to arms."

In December, Washington leased Mount Vernon from Anne, the widow of his deceased brother Lawrence, and her new husband, George Lee. For a fixed annual rental of fifteen thousand pounds of tobacco, he acquired Anne's life interest in the estate, the use of the gristmill, and the services of eighteen resident slaves. Since Anne's daughter Sarah had died, his tenure was secure as long as he paid the rent. By the terms of his brother's will, Mount Vernon would be his in fee if he survived Anne. Here was an inviting opportunity to put aside his uniform and devote his energies and abilities to the development of an ancestral place; despite his disillusioning experience with Virginia's governor, however, he was not ready to renounce a military career. At the age of twenty-three he was still very much a cavalier in the romantic tradition of an earlier age, eager to do or die for king and country. In February 1755, when he learned that Maj. Gen. Edward Braddock, newly appointed commander-in-chief of His Majesty's forces in America, had arrived in Virginia in advance of two royal regiments, he dispatched a brief note to that worthy congratulating him on his safe passage. In due course he was invited to join the general's military family as an aide, a position that would obviate any disagreeable questions of rank and precedence. It was an offer not to be resisted, an opportunity to advance his military education while retracing his route to the Ohio with a force that was committed to the recapture of Fort Duquesne and the expulsion of the French from the Ohio Valley. He politely dismissed his mother's objections and engaged his younger brother John Augustine to manage Mount Vernon in his absence.

On 1 May he joined Braddock in Frederick, Maryland, and accompanied him to Fort Cumberland, the concentration point for the combined force of regulars and colonials. There, on 10 May, it was noted in the orders of the day that "Mr. Washington is appointed Aide de Camp to His Excellency General Braddock." The march for the Ohio commenced on 7 June. Handicapped by a shortage of transport, the column moved westward through the wilderness at a snail's pace. It was handicapped also by the inability of British officers to adjust to their unaccustomed environment. The young Virginia aide found his new commander polite and congenial, but, he reported to Col. William Fairfax, the general would never give up "any point he asserts, let it be ever so incompatible with Reason."

On 9 July, as the expedition neared Fort Duquesne, the main column, about 1300 strong and mostly regulars, was ambushed by a party of 300 French and Indians. In a letter to Governor Dinwiddie, Washington reported his own remarkable survival. "I luckily escap'd with't a wound," he wrote, "tho' I had four Bullets through my Coat and two horses shot under me." The officers in general behaved bravely and suffered greatly, but there was panic, confusion, and disobedience among the British rank and file. "The Virginia Companies behav'd like Men and Died like Soldiers; for I believe out of the three Companies scarce 30 were left alive. . . . In short the dastardly behavior of the British Soldiers exposed all those who were inclined to do their duty to almost certain Death." Braddock was mortally wounded; his two regular aides were incapacitated by wounds, but escaped capture. Washington was dispatched on a desperate overnight ride to summon Colonel Dunbar and the rear guard to the support of the main force. Had there been a vigorous pursuit, there would have been few survivors, but the small attacking force was busily engaged scalping the dead and wounded and reaping a rich harvest of plunder. In a hurried note to his brother John Augustine, Washington reported "We have been most scandalously beaten by a trifling body of men." He attributed his own survival to "the miraculous care of Providence, that protected me beyond all human expectation."

BASIC TRAINING ON A GRIM FRONTIER

Braddock's defeat dealt a disastrous blow to British power in America, and the retreat of the shattered royal regiments from Fort Cumberland to Philadelphia in mid-August 1755 left the frontiers of Virginia and the adjoining provinces open to the depredations of the French and their savage allies. The House of Burgesses promptly appropriated £40000 for defense and authorized recruitment of the Virginia Regiment to full strength. Washington's reputation had been much enhanced by reports of his recent conduct under fire, and he was the obvious choice for command of this force. He was reluctant, for he was aware of difficulties that might be insurmountable; he realized, however, that Virginia was in dire straits, and he could not refuse her call, although his reputation might suffer. He was commissioned colonel and commander-in-chief of the colony's forces, with sixteen companies under him. To a friend he wrote, "I am unequal to the Task, and do assure you it requires more experience than I am master of to conduct an affair of the importance that this has now arisen to."

Twenty years later, as newly appointed commander-in-chief of the Continental army, he was to make practically the same statement to the Congress: "I do not think myself equal to the command I am honored with."

When Washington arrived at Fort Cumberland on 17 September, the garrison consisted of some 200 survivors of the Virginia companies and a company of Maryland troops under command of Capt. John Dagworthy, who had also been with Braddock. Washington was faced with a multiplicity of problems having to do with all aspects of his command: recruiting, food, clothing, arms, sanitation, drill, marksmanship, construction of forts, and, above all, discipline. Having made a beginning at the fort, the colonel set off southward with a single aide on a partial tour of the boundary he was expected to defend—300 miles of sparsely inhabited frontier extending from Fort Cumberland on the north, southward to the North Carolina line. Two thousand men, trained, well-equipped, and provisioned, would not have been equal to the task of warding off the attacks of the hostile savages, who were like wolves; yet the attempt must be made with the inadequate force that could be recruited. It would be a holding action until an expedition could once again be gathered to recapture Fort Duquesne and drive the French instigators of the savages from the Ohio Valley.

By January 1757 Washington was able to report that the Virginia frontier had suffered less than half as many casualties as had the neighboring provinces during the same period. There had been moments of panic when it seemed that the Blue Ridge might become Virginia's western boundary. The cost to the Virginia regiment in casualties had been high; in twenty engagements they had lost one third of their number.

Within the regiment there was continuing bitterness; the officers could not believe that being colonials should deprive them of "the benefits common to British subjects"; they lacked only commissions from His Majesty to make them "as regular a corps as any upon the continent." Needless to say, the bitterness of the officers over pay and privileges was shared by their commander, who in addition found himself in a dispute over rank with Captain Dagworthy, commander of the company of Maryland troops at Fort Cumberland. By virtue of an earlier commission in the British army, Dagworthy claimed jurisdiction over the fort and the mixed force of Maryland and Virginia troops that composed the garrison. In early February 1756, when it became apparent that only Governor Shirley of Massachusetts, commander of all British military forces in America, could resolve this local impasse, Colonel Washington rode off to Boston, determined to resign if he could not gain his point. On this midwinter mission of a thousand miles he traveled in high military style, with two aides and two servants, pausing en route to shop and enjoy the social amenities of Philadelphia and New York. In Boston also there were the same diversions. Governor Shirley ruled that Dagworthy took rank only as a provincial captain but did nothing about the formal petition of the officers of the Virginia Regiment for inclusion in the regular establishment.

In early September 1757 Washington's elderly friend and trusted counselor Col. William Fairfax died at Belvoir. For five crucial years Fairfax had filled the role in George Washington's life left vacant by the loss of his father and his elder half brother Lawrence, Fairfax's son-in-law. As a member of the Governor's Council, Fairfax had been well placed to advise and to mediate between his ambitious young friend and the crotchety old governor. His military experience made him a useful consultant to his friend on a wide range of problems, from the design and placement of fortifications to the procurement of supplies. There is evidence of the compatibility that existed between them in the closing of one of Fairfax's last letters to his young protegé: " . . . I am as much as any

Person can be, Dear Sir, your Affect' Friend." Belvoir, as the home of George William and Sally Fairfax, would continue to be a hospitable place of frequent resort, but the death of the patriarch left a vacancy in the small circle of George Washington's intimates that would not be filled.

In the spring of 1758, when news came of an impending expedition against Fort Duquesne under command of the British general John Forbes, there was little enthusiasm in Virginia, but for Colonel Washington it offered the prospect of an honorable release from a service that had become disagreeable to him. It was obvious that for a colonial, however talented and loyal, there was no hope of an acceptable career in the British army. He did feel a strong compulsion to retrace the route that he had twice traveled in defeat to have a part in the expulsion of the French from the Ohio and the pacification of the Indians. He would then lay aside his uniform and retire to civilian life. To one of Forbes's aides he wrote, "I have long despaired of any other reward for my Services, than the satisfaction arising from a consciousness of doing my Duty, and from the Esteem of My Friends."

With the temporary rank of brigadier, he was in command of the Virginia companies that formed a part of Forbes's force of nearly seven thousand men. The march of the army over a new road north of the old was agonizingly slow. Although the column got underway in July, it seemed that the army would be forced to go into winter quarters east of its objective. The outcome was a happy anticlimax. Interrogation of prisoners revealed that the fort was weakly held, and on 25 November an advance party discovered that the French had retreated, leaving the fort a smoldering ruin.

There was gratifying evidence of the esteem which George Washington sought in the address of the officers of the Virginia Regiment dated 31 December 1758. It was directed by twenty-seven of "his most affectionate and most obed^t humble servants" to their commander. These comrades-in-arms expressed great concern at his impending retirement. "In our earliest Infancy you took us under your Tuition, train'd us up in the Practice of that Discipline, which alone can constitute good Troops, from the punctual Observance of which you never suffer'd the least Deviation." His steady adherence to impartial justice, his quick discernment, and his invariable regard for merit had heightened their desire to emulate and to excel. "Judge then, how sensibly we must be Affected with the loss of such an excellent Commander, such a sincere Friend, and so affable a Companion. How rare is it to find those amable [*sic*] Qualifications blended together in one Man? How great the Loss of such a Man?" It is a remarkable document: a certificate of excellence. In academic terminology, it is a diploma granted by the students to their master, magna cum laude, after four rigorous years. The theatre of training was something less than continental in its dimensions, but the curriculum could scarcely have been more relevantly tailored to the challenges that destiny had in store for the graduate.

In anticipation of retirement Washington had stood for election as a burgess from Frederick County in July 1758. Although he was at the disadvantage of being detained at Fort Cumberland by duty, the candidate did not lack for local advocates. George William Fairfax and Fairfax's brother-in-law John Carlyle, an Alexandria merchant, came up from Fairfax to solicit for him, and his fellow officers in Winchester would certainly have endorsed him. The absent candidate led the poll for the two seats from Frederick by a handsome margin. His cash account reveals that his hospitality in absentia was generous: seventy-six gallons of rum, twenty-one gallons of wine, three-and-a-half gallons of brandy, and forty-six gallons of beer were dispensed. To the friend who managed this traditional election day benefaction, the victorious candidate wrote: "I am extremely thankful to you and my other Friends for entertaining the Freeholders in my name. I hope that no exceptions were taken to any that voted against me but that all were alike treated and all had enough; it was what I much desired."

On 26 February 1759 it is recorded in the official journal of the House of Burgesses that Colonel Washington "standing in his place" received the thanks of his fellow burgesses for his services and conduct in the Forbes expedition.

From neither king, ministers, nor Parliament was there ever any acknowledgment of the outstanding performance of the Virginia Regiment under its distinguished commander through all the long years of the French and Indian War. Braddock, of course, did not survive his own defeat at Monongahela long enough to officially commend the Virginia companies for their steadfastness on that occasion. In the final campaign under General Forbes, when a unit of the Virginia Regiment, at heavy cost in casualties, prevented an ill-conceived advance under Maj. James Grant of the seventy-seventh Royal Regiment from becoming a total disaster, Washington was publicly complimented by the general. But the arrogance of Grant is more characteristic of the attitude of the British officers toward their colonial compatriots. Freeman notes that this worthy is later credited with having told the House of Commons that he always treated the colonials as beasts of burden and thought they deserved no better usage because they were fit for nothing else.

It may seem idle to ponder the might-have-beens of history, but it is tempting to speculate on the course of Anglo-American relations as they might have been if George Washington had been treated as a first-class citizen and welcomed into the regular military establishment at his true worth. He might have found it more difficult to renounce his English heritage!

A Virginia Planter

George Washington and Martha Dandridge Custis, widow of Daniel Parke Custis, were married 6 January 1759. For this date we are indebted to the geneological note that Washington prepared for Sir Isaac Heard in 1792; no contemporary record of the event has come to light. The only evidence of courtship consists of three entries in the colonel's cash account for 1758, which note gratuities to Mrs. Custis's servants on two occasions in March and one in June when he stopped to

MARTHA WASHINGTON (1731–1802)

Fig. 4. A portrait by John Wollaston, painted when she was Mrs. Daniel Parke Custis.

(From the Collection of Washington and Lee University, Lexington, Virginia.)

pay his respects to their mistress in passing between Williamsburg and the frontier.

By this marriage George Washington acquired a dower interest in his wife's portion of the handsome estate that she shared with the two surviving children of her first marriage, John Parke Custis, "Jackie," age four, and his sister, Martha Parke Custis, "Patsy," age two. The real estate consisted of tobacco plantations in the Williamsburg area and one on the Eastern Shore of Virginia totaling over seventeen thousand acres, and there was personal property including slaves, livestock, securities, and accounts receivable appraised at nearly £20,000 sterling.

Lest it be assumed that the groom was a necessitous fortune hunter, we note that he did not come to the altar empty-handed. At this early stage in his career the valuation of his personal property would have been nominal, but he owned or held on lease more than 6,400 acres of land. Most important was the Mount Vernon property of just over 2100 acres on indefinite lease from Anne Washington Lee, the widow of his brother Lawrence. Here, in anticipation of his marriage, the modest villa built by his father had just been enlarged from one and one-half to two and one-half stories. In King George County near Fredericksburg he owned 1250 acres by inheritance from his father. The remainder, a total of more than 3000 acres, consisted of a 500-acre addition to the Mount Vernon leasehold and sundry tracts in Frederick and Hampshire counties, all purchased with income from his surveying and his military services.

There is abundant evidence of the domestic ease and happiness that the master of Mount Vernon enjoyed in the sixteen-year period between his homecoming with his bride in the spring of 1759 and the day in May 1775 when he rode away to attend the Second Continental Congress in Philadel-

"THE BULL-FINCH"

Fig. 5. A songbook with the name of Martha Washington and the year of their marriage in the handwriting of her husband.
(Courtesy of the Mount Vernon Ladies' Association.)

Martha Washington *1759*

THE

Bull-Finch

Being

A choice Collection

OF THE

Newest and most favourite

English Songs

Which have been

Sett to Music and Sung at

The Public Theatres & Gardens.

Printed for R. Baldwin, in Pater Noster Row,
& John Wilkie, in St. Pauls Church Yard,
LONDON.

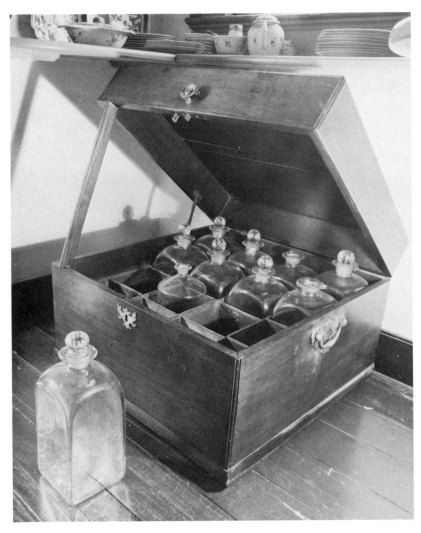

"A Neat Mahogany Square Case"

Fig. 6. In September 1760, George Washington ordered "A Neat Mahogany Square Case" from his London agent, with a request that "ye bottles be very strong." In August 1761, he protested to Robert Cary that the tradesman's charge for case and bottles, seventeen guineas, must be a mistake or "as great an imposition as ever was offered by a Tradesman." A Virginia-made case of equal quality could have been had for less than four guineas, he was certain, and he was emphatic in asserting that the bottles could not have cost thirteen guineas.

phia. His diaries, business ledgers, and correspondence afford a detailed record of his activities as a farmer-planter: his social life, recreations, and growing involvement in public affairs at the local level and at the seat of colonial government in Williamsburg. In retrospect these would loom as the happiest years of his life.

In reviewing this period, we discover the same urge to excel that had made him Virginia's outstanding military leader at the age of twenty-seven. With youthful enthusiasm he set about the task of converting a rundown plantation into a prosperous enterprise. The same talents and energies were devoted also to the management of the plantations that had been inherited by his wife and her two children. There was capital for the purchase of additional slaves and indentured servants: carpenters, a bricklayer, a blacksmith, and a gardener. There was a considerable investment in new tools and equipment. In May 1760 he bought a 2000-acre tract along the river immediately above Mount Vernon, almost doubling his local acreage. In 1761 Anne Washington Lee died, and under the terms of the will of his deceased half-brother Lawrence, his title to Mount Vernon was clear.

After four or five years of industrious devotion to the cultivation of tobacco on the several plantations under his management, the young planter discovered that his optimistic expectations were not being realized; he was, like many of his fellow planters, falling into debt to his agent. In a letter to the agent, Robert Cary & Company of London, he wrote " . . .

Washington's protest to his London agent reflects a widespread resentment among the colonists of the disadvantages under which they labored in their relations with English merchants and tradesmen. While political differences having to do with taxation played a more immediate part in the break with the mother country, this wine chest in the Mount Vernon pantry is a reminder of another very real cause of ill will among Virginia planters. These colonial Englishmen were captives of a one-crop economy and were very much at a disadvantage in their relations with the merchants in the mother country who bought their tobacco and supplied their varied needs.
(Courtesy of the Mount Vernon Ladies' Association.)

the selling of our tobacco well, and purchasing our goods upon the best terms are matters of the utmost consequence to our well doing." He was not doing well, and his complaints were frequent. He did not think that he was getting a fair price for his tobacco. All too often when the charges for freight, insurance, inspection, cartage, commission, and the heavy import duty were totaled, they exceeded the amount paid him for his consignments. On the other side of the ledger, the goods he purchased were, in his own words, "mean in quality, but not in price." He was beginning to realize that under existing trade regulations the cards were stacked against the Virginia planter. His crops could go only to England, in English vessels. Imported goods must come from the mother country; manufacturing in the colonies was discouraged by the Board of Trade. It was another instance of colonial subordination as galling as the one that had defeated his military ambitions. Instinctively he rebelled and began casting about for a way out of this economic bondage.

As a surveyor and as a soldier he had traveled widely. He was intimately familiar with the spartan life of the frontier, and he had observed the thrifty agrarian economy of the northern colonies at close range. As a first step he would restrict his patronage of London's fashionable emporiums. At Mount Vernon, where the soil was least friendly to tobacco, he would experiment with other crops. He was aware that in the Piedmont region and the more remote areas to the west, wheat was the predominant field crop. There was a good market for wheat in Alexandria. This community, in the second decade of its existence, was a thriving market town with port and shipbuilding facilities. At Mount Vernon he made a rapid transition from tobacco to wheat as his principal money crop, at the same time experimenting with hemp, flax, alfalfa, and buckwheat. He expanded his fisheries and built a new mill to grind his own grain and to do custom work for his neighbors. His carpenters doubled as coopers to make barrels for his flour and his salt herring, for both of which he found a ready market in the West Indies. He traded with Madeira for wine and with Jamaica for sugar. His domestic textile industry produced hundreds of yards of linen and woolen fabrics. By 1769 Mount Vernon had attained a high degree of self-sufficiency, and he was solvent. He could drive to Williamsburg in his chariot to attend the sessions of the House of Burgesses. George Washington and his lady were numbered among that fortunate company who, as he expressed it in a letter to his neighbor, George Mason, "live genteely and hospitably on clear estates."

TAXATION WITHOUT REPRESENTATION

In 1763 the Treaty of Paris brought the Seven Years War between England and France to a formal conclusion. News of the signing of the treaty was well received in the colonies; the sea-lanes would no longer be menaced by French men-of-war. In a letter to Cary & Co. the retired Virginia colonel wrote "We are much rejoiced at the prospect of peace, which 'tis hoped will be of long continuance and of mututal benefit to merchant and planter, as the trade to this colony will flow in a more easy and regular channel than it has done for a considerable time past." Trade did increase substantially between Britain and her North American colonies in the decade between 1763 and 1773, to the considerable benefit of the British exchequer. But the war had increased the national debt to £130,000,000; the annual carrying charge on this debt was nearly £5,000,000. In 1765 the Parliament responded to the need for greater revenues by passing the Stamp Act, requiring tax stamps on all newspapers, pamphlets, playing cards, and legal papers in the colonies.

Before the treaty of 1763 the colonies had been permitted to levy their own internal taxes without the interference of Parliament. The news of this impending tax aroused widespread indignation. In May of 1765 Patrick Henry's resolutions asserting the colonists' exclusive right to tax themselves were readily adopted by the Virginia House of Burgesses and widely circulated in the other colonies. In June the Massachusetts House of Representatives called for a colonial congress to meet and consult. Opposition to the tax was so spirited and the boycott of British goods so effective as to alarm the merchants, traders, and manufacturers at home. In response to their pleas Parliament repealed the stamp act on 18 March 1766. On the same day the king signed the Declaratory Act, which affirmed "that Parliament have, and of right ought to have, power to bind the colonies in all cases whatsoever."

George Washington was in complete accord with the feeling that the Stamp Act was an unconstitutional attack on the liberties of the colonists. In a letter to Cary & Co. dated 21 July 1766 he wrote, "The Repeal of the Stamp Act to whatsoever causes owing, ought to be much rejoiced at, for had the Parliament of Great Britain resolvd upon enforcing it the consequences I conceive would have been more direful than is generally apprehended both to the Mother Country and her Colonies. All therefore who were Instrumental in procuring the Repeal are entitled to the Thanks of every British Subject and have mine cordially."

When the Stamp Act Congress met in New York in October 1765, Virginia had not been represented, as the assembly had been prorogued by the governor and so could not name delegates. Twenty-seven delegates from nine colonies had met, remonstrated against the Stamp Act, and petitioned for its repeal. They had also declared that taxation and representation were inseparable. If the Parliament had deigned to read their petition, the colonists now had their answer in the Declaratory Act. For the moment civil disobedience in America and short-range economic interests at home had prevailed despite the fact that many members of Parliament equated rejection of the stamps with treason and rebellion. Opposition to repeal had been most obstinate in the House of Lords. There, it was reported, "the whole Bench of Bishops were for forcing the Americans to submit by fire and sword." The battle lines were drawn, and it remained to be seen whether after a brief respite the Parliament would invoke the powers asserted in the Declaratory Act, bringing to pass the direful consequences apprehended by George Washington.

In the summer of 1767 the British Parliament implemented

the powers asserted the previous year by passing the Townshend Acts, so called in honor of the chancellor of the Exchequer. One of these acts imposed a duty to be collected in the colonies on glass, paper, paint pigments, and tea. Even more ominous was a provision suspending the New York Assembly until it should rescind its action denying salt, vinegar, and cider or beer to British troops quartered in that province. In April 1768, the Virginia Assembly once again addressed memorials and remonstrances to king and Parliament. Of more consequence was the assembly's acknowledgment of a "circular letter" received from the Massachusetts House applauding that body's sentiments and urging unified opposition by all the colonies to every attack on their liberties.

It would be difficult on the basis of the surviving record to determine the exact point of no return in George Washington's relations with the mother country—the moment of ultimate disillusionment and alienation. There was a possible occasion of final rejection in the autumn of 1768, when he spent a week or more in Williamsburg. Virginia's new governor, Lord Botetourt, had just arrived. His attitude was conciliatory. He was under secret instructions to reason with the councillors and other Virginia leaders in an attempt to persuade them to accept the principle of the supremacy of Parliament. (His instructions also authorized him to call for military assistance from the general commanding in North America in case of civil commotion.) Washington's diary notes that he attended a reception for the new governor on 31 October and a dinner in his honor on 2 November. It is possible that on one of these occasions or at some unrecorded moment the new governor, recognizing Washington as a desirable political convert, attempted to bring him into the fold. The record is silent; if he tried, of course, he failed.

Any doubt of this point would be stilled by Washington's letter of 5 April 1769 to his neighbor George Mason, enclosing papers that he had just received from a correspondent in Maryland. These papers proposed an organized boycott of British goods so long as Parliament attempted to impose taxes on the colonists or suppressed colonial assemblies. Washing-

GEORGE MASON (1725–92)

Fig. 7. An early-nineteenth-century copy of a portrait by Hesselius, ca.
1750
(Courtesy of S. Cooper Dawson, Jr., a direct descendant of George Mason.)

ton's letter to Mason is poorly composed and awkward in
style, but on several points it is crystal clear: "No man should
scruple, or hesitate" to take up arms in defense of his heredi-
tary liberties, he wrote. Addresses to the throne and remonstrances to Parliament have proven their inefficacy. It remains only to be determined whether "starving their trades
and manufactures" will be effective, before appealing to arms
as a last resort. There is no hint of compromise with "our

lordly Masters in Great Britain"; no man should scruple or hestiate to take the final step!

When Washington arrived in Williamsburg in early May to attend a meeting of the assembly, he had with him Mason's draft of a proposed association that would bind all signatories not to import a long list of British goods. Before considering this proposal, the House of Burgesses adopted resolutions reasserting its exclusive right to levy taxes in Virginia and condemning the recent Parliament's proposal to transport colonists accused of treason to England for trial. On the following day the House incorporated these resolves in a humble address to the king. For this presumption it was promptly dissolved by the governor.

Immediately after their dismissal, most of the burgesses reconvened at the Raleigh Tavern and adopted articles of association incorporating most of Mason's suggestions. Eighty-eight burgesses, a three-fourths majority of the House, signed the final document.

After new elections, the General Assembly convened on 7 November to be assured by the governor that His Majesty's administration would propose elimination of all taxes save the one on tea "such duties having been laid contrary to the true principles of commerce." The burgesses were not entirely appeased by this partial repeal, but the association languished and was finally abandoned in July 1771.

For the more dedicated colonial patriots, tea remained on the forbidden list, but the customs record on tea imports indicates widespread public indifference or forgetfulness. Had the Parliament been content to relax, the truce might have been prolonged indefinitely, but in May 1773 that body was so ill-advised as to grant the East India Company what was in effect an empire-wide monopoly of the tea trade. The company was free to bypass regular mercantile channels and to collect the duty in the colonies through its own outlets. It could undersell even the smuggled leaf. Militant patriots found themselves in active alliance with injured merchants and traders. In Boston on the night of 16 December 1773 Sons of Liberty disguised as Indians dumped 342 chests of the East India Company's tea into the harbor. In retaliation Parliament passed the Boston Port Bill and other repressive measures.

On 24 May the House of Burgesses, responding to news of the Boston Port Bill, resolved that the date of closing of the port, 1 June, should be a day of fasting, humiliation, and prayer. Two days later, Governor Dunmore dissolved the assembly. Once again the burgesses reconvened at Raleigh Tavern to form an association and to recommend another boycott. Declaring that an attack on one colony was an attack on all British America, they called for a general congress that would meet annually. Three days later twenty-five burgesses who were still in the area met to consider an appeal from the Boston Committee of Correspondence for more specific measures. A convention was summoned to meet in Williamsburg on 1 August 1774.

"CAN A VIRTUOUS MAN HESITATE?"

The feelings of the senior burgess from Fairfax at this critical period are freely expressed in a letter to his intimate friend and neighbor George William Fairfax who with his lady had sailed for England the previous summer to settle an estate. From Williamsburg on 10 June 1774, Washington wrote:

The Ministry may rely on it that Americans will never be tax'd without their own consent that the cause of Boston the despotick Measures in respect to it I mean now is and ever will be considered as the cause of America (not that we approve their conduct in destroyg. the Tea) and that we shall not suffer ourselves to be sacrificed by piece meals though god only knows what is to become of us, threatned as we are with so many hoverg. evils as hang over us at present; having a cruel and blood thirsty Enemy upon our Backs, the Indians, between whom and our Frontier Inhabitants many Skirmishes have happnd, and with whom a general War is inevitable whilst those from whom we have a right to seek protection are endeavouring by every piece of Art and despotism to fix the Shackles of Slavery upon us.

GEORGE WILLIAM FAIRFAX (1725–83)

Fig. 8. A portrait painted after his return to England in 1773 by an un-identified artist.
(Courtesy of Mrs. Charles Baird, Jr.)

37

At the August convention, Washington was one of seven members elected to represent Virginia at the Continental Congress that was to convene in Philadelphia on 5 September. That body created a continental association and established uniform dates for nonintercourse with the mother country. There was no threat of war; nor was there hint of compromise. Force would be met with force, and arrests would provoke reprisals.

On 9 October from Philadelphia, Washington acknowledged a letter from Robert MacKenzie, a fellow veteran of the Virginia Regiment who was now a British regular officer attached to a regiment stationed in Boston. MacKenzie had criticized the turbulent and lawless conduct of the Bostonians, their "fixed aim at total independence." Washington's reply reflects the views and the spirit of the delegates with whom he is meeting. It is not the wish of any colony "to set up for independency," he wrote, "Give me leave to add as my opinion that more blood will be spilt on this occasion, if the ministry are determined to push matters to extremity than history has yet furnished instances of in the annals of North America."

In March 1775 Washington attended a second convention, which had been called to consider measures of defense and to select delegates who would represent Virginia at the Second Continental Congress, scheduled to convene in Philadelphia on 10 May. This time the convention met in the infant community of Richmond to avoid possibility of interference should a British man-of-war enter Chesapeake Bay by chance or by invitation of Governor Dunmore. On the day after Patrick Henry had issued his dramatic call to arms, Washington wrote to his brother John Augustine, who was training an independent company in Westmoreland County: "I have promised to review the Independent Company of Richmond [county], some time this summer, they having made me a tender of the command of it. At the same time I could review yours and shall very cheerfully accept the honor of commanding it if occasion requires it to be drawn out, as it is my full intention to devote my life and fortune in the cause we are engaged in, if need be."

At the end of May Washington wrote again to his absent Belvoir neighbor, this time from Philadelphia. His letter carried tidings of the fighting at Concord and Lexington. The British expedition had been fortunate to escape, Washington wrote. The initiative and spirit of the Minutemen were gratifying, but the outlook was ominous. He continued, "Unhappy it is, though, to reflect that a brother's sword has been sheathed in a brother's breast and that the once happy and peaceful plains of American are either to be drenched in blood or inhabited by slaves. Sad alternative! But can a virtuous man hesitate in his choice?" The making of a rebel had come to full fruition. "Can a virtuous man hesitate?" At the moment of composition the question was rhetorical, but a few days later the retired Virginia colonel, in an exalted setting, would respond to it!

June 16, 1775

Mr. President: Tho' I am truly sensible of the high Honour done me in this Appointment, yet I feel great distress from a consciousness that my abilities and Military experience may not be equal to the extensive and important Trust: However, as the Congress desires I will enter upon the momentous duty, and exert every power I Possess In their Service for the Support of the glorious Cause: I beg they will accept my most cordial thanks for this distinguished testimony of their Approbation.

But lest some unlucky event should happen unfavourable to my reputation, I beg it may be remembered by every Gentn. in the room, that I this day declare with the utmost sincerity, I do not think my self equal to the Command I am honoured with.

As to pay, Sir, I beg leave to Assure the Congress that as no pecuniary consideration could have tempted me to have accepted this Arduous employment [at the expence of my domestt. ease and happiness] I do not wish to make any profitt from it: I will keep an exact Account of my expences; those I doubt not they will discharge and that is all I desire.

PART II

Leader of the Revolution

Leader of the Revolution

"A Kind of Destiny"

It must indeed have seemed to George Washington that a kind of destiny had forced him over the Rubicon as he sat down to report to Mrs. Washington that he had accepted military leadership of the armed resistance to the mother country:

Philadelphia, June 18, 1775

My Dearest: I am now set down to write to you on a subject, which fills me with inexpressible concern, and this concern is greatly aggravated and increased, when I reflect upon the uneasiness I know it will give you. It has been determined in Congress, that the whole army raised for the defence of the American cause shall be put under my care, and that it is necessary for me to proceed immediately to Boston to take upon me the command of it.

You may believe me, my dear Patsy, when I assure you, in the most solemn manner that, so far from seeking this appointment, I have used every endeavor in my power to avoid it, not only from my unwillingness to part with you and the family, but from a consciousness of its being a trust too great for my capacity, and that I should enjoy more real happiness in one month with you at home, than I have the most distant prospect of finding abroad, if my stay were to be seven times seven years. But as it has been a kind of destiny, that has thrown me upon this service, I shall hope that my undertaking it is designed to answer some good purpose. You might, and I suppose did perceive, from the tenor of my letters, that I was apprehensive I could not avoid the appointment, as I did

43

not pretend to intimate when I should return. That was the case. It was utterly out of my power to refuse this appointment, without exposing my character to such censures, as would have reflected dishonor upon myself, and given pain to my friends. This, I am sure, could not, and ought not, to be pleasing to you, and must have lessened me considerably in my own esteem. I shall rely, therefore, confidently on that Providence, which has heretofore preserved and been bountiful to me, not doubting but that I shall return safe to you in the fall. I shall feel no pain from the toil or the danger of the campaign; my unhappiness will flow from the uneasiness I know you will feel from being left alone. I therefore beg, that you will summon your whole fortitude, and pass your time as agreeably as possible. Nothing will give me so much sincere satisfaction as to hear this, and to hear it from your own pen. My earnest and ardent desire is, that you would pursue any plan that is most likely to produce content, and a tolerable degree of tranquillity; as it must add greatly to my uneasy feelings to hear, that you are dissatisfied or complaining at what I really could not avoid.

As life is always uncertain, and common prudence dictates to every man the necessity of settling his temporal concerns, while it is in his power, and while the mind is calm and undisturbed, I have, since I came to this place (for I had not time to do it before I left home) got Colonel Pendleton to draft a will for me, by the directions I gave him, which will I now enclose. The provision made for you in case of my death will, I hope, be agreeable.

I shall add nothing more, as I have several letters to write, but to desire that you will remember me to your friends, and to assure you that I am, with the most unfeigned regard, my dear Patsy, your affectionate, &c. George Washington

This carefully measured statement of a troubled man to his most intimate and most concerned confidante covered many points. "So far from seeking this appointment, I have used every effort in my power to avoid it." The Virginia colonel had taken his uniform, presumably the one he had worn in the French and Indian War, to Philadelphia and had worn it daily. To some latter-day commentators, this appearance in military garb and his frequently expressed belligerence have suggested that he was electioneering for high military office. This conclusion is understandable, but it is based on something less than a careful appraisal of the circumstances. At this moment in his career George Washington thought of himself as a Virginian, and like many of his fellow Virginians, he thought and wrote of Virginia as "my Country." Before leaving for Philadelphia he had been asked by three, perhaps more, of the newly formed volunteer military units in northern and eastern Virginia to be their commander. He had been commissioned to procure uniforms in Philadelphia for one of them. It was quite natural that at this point he would have envisioned returning to Virginia to command all of the military forces that might be raised there. He would have been untroubled by any sense of a higher allegiance to an oppressing mother country. On the contrary, he would have risen to the challenge of such a command, relishing the thought of leading an infantry composed of frontiersmen with their long rifles, together with his Tidewater compatriots mounted on their blooded horses, against invading redcoats. But he must have been deeply troubled by the prospect of going among a people who were to him unknown, to displace their own local leader. Certain it is that his renunciation of salary in his acceptance speech and his statement that he did not feel himself equal to the command were directed to fellow delegates who were aware of his reluctance.

"I should enjoy more real happiness in one month with you at home, than I have the most distant prospect of finding abroad, if my stay were to be seven times seven years." Here is an evidence of the real George Washington, a man truly content with his life as husband and husbandman on the bank of the Potomac. There is evidence here of the fulfillment of an expectation he had voiced to a London correspondent in 1759: "I am now I believe fixd at this Seat with an agreable Consort for Life and hope to find more happiness in retirement than I ever experienc'd amidst a wide and bustling World." Fifteen years of domestic felicity had been granted him. This and something more; he and his amiable consort were among that select group of Virginians whom he had described in his letter of April 1769 to George Mason as those who lived "genteelly and hospitably on clear estates." This high and enviable state of well-being had been rudely interrupted; the golden years at Mount Vernon had come to an abrupt end.

"It was utterly out of my power to refuse this appointment." His honor was involved, his self-esteem. And something more, an inability he had confessed to his neighbor, John West, in January when he declined to act as the administrator of his estate. "I never deny, or even hesitate in granting any request that is made to me," he wrote, "(especially by persons I esteem and in matters of moment) without a feeling of in expressable uneasiness." This statement, one of the most self-revealing to be found in the many volumes of George Washington's writings, foretold the decision he would make in Philadelphia five months later, uneasily and reluctantly. It was indeed a matter of moment, for himself and for posterity.

He would, he wrote, rely on that Providence that had previously been bountiful to him. Experience indicated the existence of a beneficent Supreme Being who had brought him unscathed through the Battle of Monongahela twenty years earlier, when two horses had been shot out from under him and his clothing had been pierced by bullets; of a Providence that had spared him all the dire potentialities he had hazarded during two years as commander of the Virginia Regiment, defending the frontier. A fatalistic belief in "Destiny" that had governed his earlier years had been transformed into a faith in Providence, which might not see him safely home in the fall but would bring him unharmed through the looming perils.

And yet, "as life is always uncertain," he had a will drawn. Here we read between the lines; random disasters do occur despite that overruling Providence. This was probably his first will, and there is no record of another until the summer of 1799, when he drew up the one that became his final testament. At this moment in Philadelphia, prudence, as he noted, certainly dictated the drawing of a will, and for a more specific reason than those he mentioned. He was about to go into combat against his mother country, the most formidable military power in the world. He might well die in battle, or as a captured rebel at the end of a rope.

Letters of announcement went also to his stepson, John Parke Custis, to Burwell Bassett, husband of Mrs. Washington's sister, Anna Maria, and to the brother closest in his affections, John Augustine Washington. If there were other letters to family or intimate friends on this occasion, they have not come to light. In the midst of hurried preparations for the journey to Cambridge, there would have been little time for correspondence.

The language of the newly commissioned general to these three relatives by blood or marriage differed, but the letters were all in the same vein. Of the three addresses, young Custis was probably uppermost in the writer's mind. He had been something of a problem child for his stepfather, who once wrote that the lad's interests tended more strongly to dogs, horses, and guns than to book knowledge. His tutor, Jonathan Boucher, had written to the stepfather, "I never did in my life know a youth so exceedingly indolent or so surprisingly voluptuous." In 1774 at the age of nineteen, Jackie had dropped out of Kings College in New York to marry Eleanor Calvert, daughter of Benedict Calvert of Mount Airy, Maryland. One of ten children, the bride brought a small dowry; she was of distinguished lineage, however, and George Washington with good grace concealed his misgivings about the tender age of bride and groom and his disappointment at the latter's renunciation of higher education.

The letter to Bassett also had more immediacy than did the one to his brother John. Bassett's wife, Anna Maria, and her sister, Martha, were closely tied by family association and mutual devotion. The Bassetts lived at Eltham on the bank of the Pamunkey River near Williamsburg. Bassett was a member of the House of Burgesses. If we may judge by the number of entries in Washington's prewar diaries, the Bassetts were his most congenial relatives and Eltham was his favorite home away from home as he journeyed to and from Williamsburg to attend the meetings of the House of Burgesses. On these periodic journeys Mrs. Washington was usually left at Eltham with her sister and brother-in-law.

According to George Washington Parke Custis—Martha Washington's grandson—John Augustine Washington, "Brother Jack," was the general's favorite brother. Other testimony confirms the lifelong intimacy between the two men. In their bachelor days they had spent much time together at Mount Vernon. During his older brother's absence with Braddock and later as commander of the Virginia Regiment, Brother Jack had managed the Mount Vernon estate. John Augustine had married Hannah Bushrod of Westmoreland County. They lived at Bushfield, the bride's heritage, at the mouth of Nomini Creek, overlooking the broad Potomac. "The house," wrote Fithian, tutor to the children of Robert Carter at nearby Nomini Hall, "has the most agreeable situation I have yet seen in Maryland or Virginia." The Bushfield establishment was quite modest by comparison with Nomini Hall and nearby Stratford, seat of the Lees, or with Mount Airy, the Tayloe home in adjoining Richmond County, but John Augustine's ledger and assessors' lists confirm that his holdings ranked him among the first ten landowners in Westmoreland County. He was a vestryman in his parish, with all the church and civil responsibilities that attached. He was a colonel, commanding local militia, and a member of the Westmoreland County Committee, one of those bodies of leading men in each Virginia county that functioned so effectively during the difficult period of transition from colony to statehood. His sphere was smaller and more remote than that of the Lees, who spoke and acted to such effect at state and national levels, but he was a man of distinction in a community that was noteworthy for the number and brilliance of its public-spirited men.

To Jackie, Washington wrote that his appointment was an honor he neither sought "or was by any means fond of accepting." To Bassett, it was an honor he had wished to avoid. To the latter he spelled out three constants: "I can answer but for three things, a firm belief in the justice of our Cause, close attention in the prosecution of it, and the strictest integrity."

In each letter he emphasized his concern for Mrs. Washington's welfare. Young Custis and his wife were urged to abide at Mount Vernon; this, the general wrote, was "absolutely necessary for the peace and satisfaction" of Mrs. Washington. The Bassetts must visit Mount Vernon, if possible, and take Mrs. Washington home with them to New Kent County for a summer sojourn. John Augustine and his wife must find leisure during the summer to "spend a little time" at Mount Vernon, "although the distance is great." This concern of an absent husband for his wife was not unfounded. Mrs. Washington was forty-five, perhaps not in the best of health. Two years earlier she had lost an only daughter, Patsy, who had died of epilepsy after a long series of seizures. Jackie and his bride were now seeking land on which to establish their home, but this plan must be held in abeyance, since George Washington, as he "imbarked upon a tempestuous Ocean," could not allow his wife to be left alone on an isolated plantation if it could be avoided.

"Not doubting but that I shall return safe to you in the fall." This affirmation in the letter of 18 June to Martha was repeated in modified form as George Washington penned a farewell note from Philadelphia five days later, a few minutes before setting out for Cambridge: "in full confidence of a happy meeting with you some time in the fall." A time limit must be placed on her acceptance of this period of separation and anxiety, even though reason would qualify the assurance. No doubt George Washington did hope to return home in the autumn and would have avoided contemplating a longer absence, which would be not only contrary to inclination but also injurious to his private interests.

"The Only Comfortable Reflection"

Notice of concern about his private affairs is strangely absent in the surviving letters written from Philadelphia on the eve of Washington's departure for Cambridge. A letter or let-

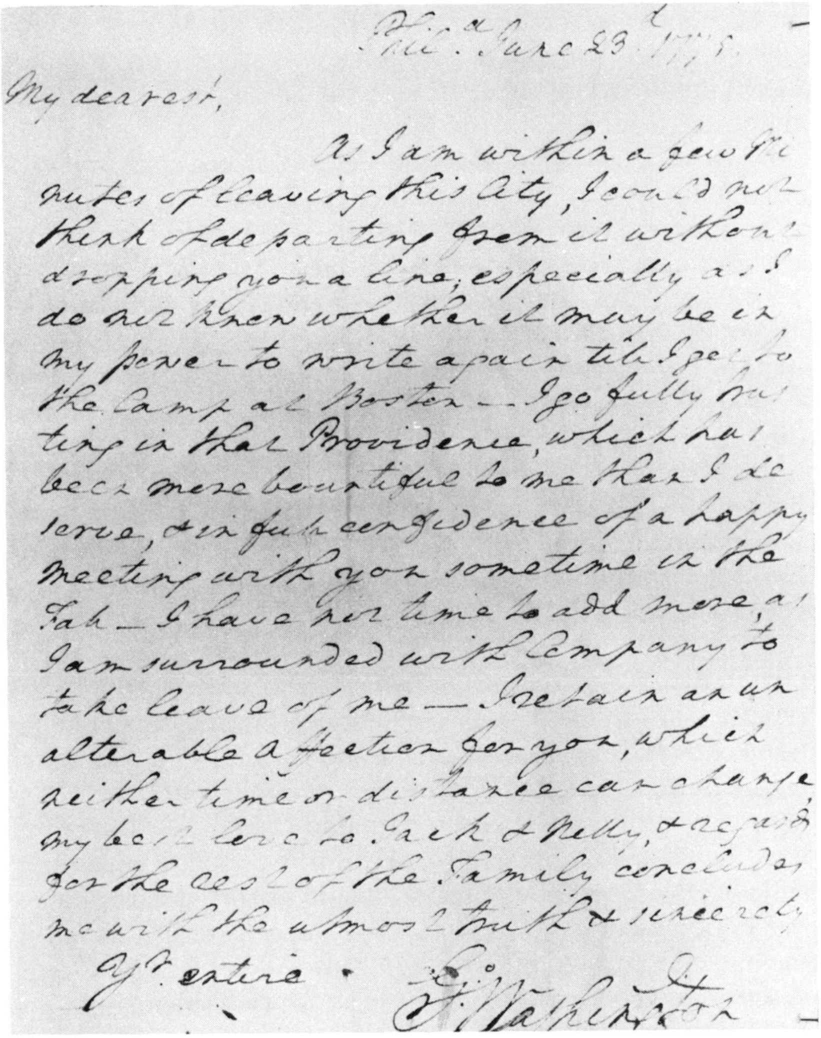

Phila. June 23d 1775.

My dearest,

As I am within a few mi=
nutes of leaving this City, I could not
think of departing from it without
dropping you a line, especially as I
do not know whether it may be in
my power to write again till I get to
the Camp at Boston — I go fully be=
lieving in that Providence, which has
been more bountiful to me than I de=
serve, & in full confidence of a happy
meeting with you sometime in the
Fall — I have not time to add more, as
I am surrounded with Company to
take leave of me — I retain an un
alterable affection for you, which
neither time or distance can change
my best love to Jack & Nelly, & regard
for the rest of the Family; concludes
me with the utmost truth & sincerity,
Yr entire
Go Washington

"YR ENTIRE G⁰ WASHINGTON"

Fig. 9. The newly appointed commander-in-chief is about to ride off to
Cambridge. Members of Congress have gathered to see him off, a band
is playing, and members of the Philadelphia Light Horse will escort him
on the first stage of his journey.
(Courtesy of the Mount Vernon Ladies' Association.)

MARTHA WASHINGTON'S DESK

Fig. 10. This was one of several pieces of furniture purchased by President Washington from the French minister for his official residence in New York. The desk was inherited by Mrs. Washington's granddaughter and namesake, Martha Parke Custis Peter. According to family tradition, Mrs. Peter found hidden away in a recess of the desk General Washington's two letters of June 1775 to her grandmother. These two letters, deliberately spared or overlooked, are the only known survivors of Mrs. Washington's destruction of her correspondence with her husband. The original of the letter of June 23 is in the Mount Vernon Collection. *(Courtesy of the Mount Vernon Ladies' Association.)*

ters to his manager, Lund Washington, would have been indicated, not only by business necessity but also by the long-established ties of friendship and close associations which existed between them.

In a letter to Lafayette in 1781, General Washington stated that he had "lived in perfect intimacy for near 20 Years" with Lund Washington. They were third cousins, as George was a great grandson of the emigrant John Washington and Lund a great grandson of Lawrence—John's brother and fellow-emigrant. Lund was George's junior by five years; he was born on his father's plantation near the mouth of Chotank Creek, a tributary of the Potomac, in King George County, Virginia, in 1737. Lund had three brothers, two of whom survived George Washington and were remembered in his will as "acquaintances and friends of my Juvenile years, Lawrence Washington & Robert Washington of Chotank." This would indicate an early acquaintance with Lund also, but at a time of life when a difference of five years in age would have inhibited active companionship. The year 1743 had a common significance for George and Lund; in that year each was left in the sole custody of his mother by the death of a father.

Of Lund's education and early career there is no record. His personal ledger indicates that he was employed by one Edward Carter in the early 1760s. It appears from the same source that he was building a mill for William Fitzhugh in Fairfax County during 1763 and part of 1764. In October 1764, he entered the service of George Washington and became a resident of Mount Vernon. His position corresponded to that of steward on a large English estate, qualified perhaps by the fact that his employer was more active in the management of his own affairs than were most proprietors. Lund was George Washington's business agent, assistant manager of Mount Vernon when the master was in residence and in charge in his absence, and he was frequently sent on business missions with full power to act for his principal. Prior to the Revolution his compensation, based on the value of crops made, averaged about ninety pounds a year. A bachelor, he was a member of the household and participated fully in the social life of the family. Fortune had denied him the common heritage of a young Virginian of his day—a landed estate—and while this lack might handicap him in pursuit of matrimony, it did not impair his social position.

In mid-October 1775 Lund acknowledged receipt of ten letters from the general since his departure from Philadelphia, only one of which survives. Although he does not mention the earlier period in Philadelphia, the inference would be that a regular correspondence had been inaugurated on General Washington's arrival there. In any case, the master of Mount Vernon did not accept the reality of prolonged absence until early October, when he wrote to Mrs. Washington inviting her to join him at headquarters. It was not until November that he faced the prospect of indefinite exile in relation to his business affairs and wrote to Lund on this score. The original letter is missing, but it survives in part through a partial copy annotated and retained by the writer, as will appear below:

November 26, 1775.

What follows is a part of a letter wrote to Mr. Lund Washington the 26th. day of November 1775. A Copy is taken to remind me of my engagements and the exact purport of them. These paragraphs follow an earnest request to employ good part of my force in cleaning up Swamps, H. Hole Ditching, Hedging &c.

"I well know where the difficulty of accomplishing these things will lie. Overseers are already engaged (upon shares) to look after my business. Remote advantages to me, however manifest and beneficial, are nothing to them; and to engage standing Wages, when I do not know that anything I have, or can raise, will command Cash, is attended with hazard; for which reason I hardly know what more to say than to discover my wishes. The same reason, although it may in appearance have the same tendency in respect to you, shall not be same in its operation. For I will engage for the Year coming, and the year following, that if these troubles, and my absence continues, that your Wages shall be standing and certain, at the highest amount that any one Year's Crop has produced to you yet. I do not offer this as any temptation to induce *you* to go on more chearfully in prosecuting *these* schemes of *mine*. I should do injustice to you, were I not to acknowledge that your

53

conduct has ever appeared to me, above every thing sordid; but I offer it in consideration of the great charge you have upon your hands, and my entire dependance upon your fidelity and industry.

"It is the greatest, indeed it is the only comfortable reflexion I enjoy on this score, to think that my business is in the hands of a person in whose integrity I have not a doubt, and on whose care I can rely. Was it not for this, I should feel very unhappy on Account of the situation of my affairs; but I am persuaded you will do for me as you would for yourself, and more than this I cannot expect.

"Let the Hospitality of the House, with respect to the poor, be kept up; Let no one go hungry away. If any of these kind of People should be in want of Corn, supply their necessities, provided it does not encourage them in idleness; and I have no objection to your giving my Money in Charity, to the Amount of forty or fifty Pounds a Year, when you think it well bestowed. What I mean, by having no objection, is, that it is my desire that it should be done. You are to consider that neither myself or Wife are now in the way to do these good Offices. In all other respects, I recommend it to you, and have no doubts, of your observing the greatest Oeconomy and frugality; as I suppose you know that I do not get a farthing for my services here more than my Expenses; It becomes necessary, therefore, for me to be saving at home."

The above is copied, not only to remind myself of my promises, and requests; but others, also, if any mischance happens to G. Washington.

Lund made no acknowledgment of this letter until he was reminded of his omission. He then wrote (15 February 1776):

Your letter of January 25th [not extant] has come to hand. If I neglected to answer your letter of the 26th of November, relative to my wages, it was not intentionally. I should be very sorry that you should believe that I would exact more of you now, than when you lived at home. Had you not offered to pay me equal to what I had in any former year, I should not have murmured; but cheerfully endeavored to have executed your orders with regard to hedging, meadowing, etc. If my mind had been set on riches, I very probably should have been trying every year that I have lived with you, to get more of you. You will do me the justice to say that I have made no such attempt. God forbid I should at this time do it, when you have it scarcely in your power to refuse me. I never expect to be rich, my only wish or ambition has been to save so much out of my wages during the time I have served you and others, as would be sufficient to purchase a small farm in some part of the country, where the produce of it would enable me to live and give a neighbor beef and toddy. But that I now despair of every accomplishing on this side of the Allegheny mountains, for my own employment is such that I cannot do you justice, and run about the country to look where such a purchase may be made. But no more; my affairs are to myself and why should I pester you with them. You may be assured my whole time and thoughts shall be devoted to your service, and as to any extraordinary care or trouble I am at, I think nothing of it, for it is a maxim with me, that he who receives the wages of another, hath no time which he in right can call his own.

This exchange constituted the informal agreement by which Lund Washington managed Mount Vernon until the general retired to private life in December 1783. It was an agreement between gentlemen, and it is manifest from Lund's belated acknowledgment of General Washington's statement that he felt this exchange of assurances to be superfluous.

A LARGE VIRGINIA ESTATE

George Washington was fortunate in having an honest and conscientious kinsman, experienced in his methods and thoroughly conversant with his business affairs, to carry on at Mount Vernon in his absence. The responsibility of managing a large Virginia estate, a heavy and exacting one at best, was now to be intensified by the exigencies of a wartime economy. With markets disrupted or closed and no assurance of income from crops, debtors evading their obligations and creditors pressing their claims, Lund must carry on. Commerce was at a standstill, scarce commodities were being hoarded, yet a resident population of nearly two hundred must be fed, clothed, sheltered, and maintained in health.

The Mount Vernon inhabitants were divided between the "Home House" and four adjoining farms or plantations. At this period George Washington used the designations "farm" and "plantation" interchangeably, perhaps because he had been in process of transition from the cultivation of tobacco, a crop which was planted by hand and cultivated with hand tools, to field cropping. Wheat had been substituted for tobacco as a money crop and he was constantly experimenting in search of a profitable diversification of his farming operation. The number of field crops he raised, attempted to raise, or at least tested on a small scale is said to have been well above sixty. These included barley, clover, corn, flax, millet, oats, orchard grass, timothy, lucerne, and wheat. In later years he was wont to identify himself as a farmer or husbandman and on the map he drew in 1793, the units of his Mount Vernon estate were identified as farms.

Two hundred seems a conservative estimate of the number of persons domiciled at Mount Vernon in 1775. An official Fairfax County census in 1782 lists one hundred and eighty-eight blacks, by far the largest number for any farm or plantation in the county. In the General's diary for 1786, when he was in full-time residence and actively managing his local enterprise, there is a very precise enumeration of the slave population; by that time it numbered two hundred and sixteen. At the beginning of the Revolution Lund was responsible for a smaller number, but the proportions in terms of age and sex would have been quite similar; the organization and distribution of the adults about the place would have varied little.

The Home House appears first in the 1786 tabulation, and Billy Lee heads the list. He is identified as "val de chambre." In this capacity he had gone to Philadelphia with his master in the spring of 1775 and served faithfully through all the years of the war, from Cambridge to Yorktown and back to Mount Vernon two years later, when the general at last returned his commission to the Congress. Before the war Billy had doubled as body servant and huntsman when Washington took to the fields with the Mount Vernon foxhounds. Two waiters and two cooks, all male, are next listed, followed by three drivers and stablers. There were two women almost past service and three "sempstresses." The latter would have made clothes for their fellow workers from coarse imported material or from cloth woven on the place. One more skilled might have sewed for the immediate family under Mrs. Washington's direction. There were two housemaids and two laundresses, four spinners (one almost blind). There was a stockkeeper and an "old jobber." Seven laborers, a waggoner, a carter, and a gardener are listed, in that order. There were four carpenters and two smiths. Last on the list was a lame knitter, Peter. There were twenty-six children, making a total of sixty-seven blacks at the Home House.

The mill was an important appendage of the establishment. It ground the Mount Vernon wheat and corn and did custom work for a wide neighborhood. Nicholas Cresswell, a young Englishman who was aboard a small schooner that stopped to load flour in 1774, noted that the mill was very complete and made "as good flour as I ever saw." William Roberts was in charge. His employer held him in high regard as an honest man and one who understood "the manufacture of wheat as well as any miller upon the Continent." Unfortunately Roberts had a weakness for strong drink. The 1786 tabulation lists one black miller and three coopers here. These coopers made barrels for flour and for the shad and herring that were netted in the Potomac each spring. They also made a variety of utensils for all the farms—churns, tubs, piggins, pails, and kegs.

At River Farm there was a black overseer with a working staff of ten men and seven women. The overseer's wife is listed separately, indicating that she was exempt from working in the fields. There were twenty-two children, making a total of fifty-one persons on this plantation, the largest of the five farms about the mansion house.

Dogue Run Farm also had a black overseer. There were eight active laboring men and one disabled. A nonlaboring overseer's wife and ten laboring women, plus one who was superannuated, completed the adult roll here. There were seventeen children, for a total here of thirty-eight.

At Ferry Farm there were five laboring men and ten laboring women. Fifteen children brought the total here to thirty.

Muddy Hole Farm also had a black overseer. There were five laboring men, nine laboring women, and eleven children, for a total population—according to the diarist, whom we would be loath to fault—of twenty-five.

It is noted that of this total Mount Vernon population of 216, 109 were "dower" Negroes, that is, acquired by George Washington's marriage to Martha Custis, or children of the females acquired by that marriage.

In 1775 Lund's white assistants, in addition to Roberts, included Thomas Bishop, an elderly Englishman who functioned as overseer at the Home House. Bishop had been George Washington's servant during the French and Indian War and entered service at Mount Vernon not long after. He lived in a cottage with his wife and daughter not far from the mansion, secure under the benevolent protection of his patron. His abilities as an overseer were modest, and his responsibilities were limited accordingly. Mrs. Bishop was the Mount Vernon midwife.

Among Lund's other white aides was John Alton, another elderly retainer who had been long in service and who appears also to have been an overseer of modest abilities. He lived on and served through the war period, dying as overseer of River Farm in 1785.

There was Bateman, the gardener, who seems to have settled in quite comfortably. "I have no expectation of his ever seeking another home," wrote Lund to his employer in 1783. "Indulge him but in getting drunk now and then and he will be happy. He is the best kitchen gardener to be met with." In time of war vegetables and herbs were more important than ornamentals.

In April of 1775 William Webster, a brickmaker from Scotland, and Tom Spears, a carpenter from England, both indentured, had made off in their master's small yawl. Spears seems to have made good his escape, but in October Webster was back at Mount Vernon and, by Lund's report, making brick once again. Caleb Stone, another indentured servant, was boss carpenter.

The names of three journeyman workers appear in the records of the Revolutionary period, each in part- or full-time capacity. James Boyd was a shoemaker; in May of 1775 he was credited also with shearing 403 sheep. Andrew Judge was a tailor and William Keating a weaver. These men would have been paid on a piecework basis. Later, as state and continental currencies lost value, they may have been paid in kind—cornmeal, salt fish, or cured meat from the Mount Vernon smokehouse.

The master of Mount Vernon most commonly referred to his slaves as "the Negroes," or "my people." Those in residence about the mansion, when referred to collectively, were identified as "servants"; the other principal category, the workers on the outlying farms, were referred to as "the hands." Whites under indenture appear in the record as "white servants." There is evidence of an effort to minimize intermingling of the races in the designation of a mansion wing building as "the white servants hall," as well as in the existence of a white servants kitchen in the mansion basement.

During the Revolution and earlier the majority of the Negroes at the mansion were domiciled in a "house for families" just east of the flower garden. This was a substantial two-story frame structure, much superior to the huts or cabins that housed the workers on the out-farms. It would be replaced after the war by the servants quarters, the one-story brick wings of the new greenhouse.

The journal of Julian Niemcewicz, the Polish traveler who visited Mount Vernon in 1798, records a description of Negro family dwellings on one of the Mount Vernon farms. He writes:

We entered some negroes' huts—for their habitations cannot be called houses. They are far more miserable than the poorest of the cottages of our peasants. The husband and his wife sleep on a miserable bed, the children on the floor. A very poor chimney, a little kitchen furniture amid this misery—a tea kettle and cups. . . . A small orchard with vegetables was situated close to the hut. Five or six hens, each with ten or fifteen chickens walked there. This is the

HOUSE FOR FAMILIES

Fig. 11. From a 1792 painting by an unidentified artist. This wooden structure was razed in 1792. To its right appears a section of one of the wings of the greenhouse. These single-story brick units replaced the house for families as quarters for the black servants domiciled at the mansion house.
(Courtesy of the Mount Vernon Ladies' Association.)

only pleasure allowed to negroes; they are not permitted to keep either ducks or geese or pigs. They sell the chickens in Alexandria and buy with the money some furniture.

From the Mount Vernon domestic writings of a slightly earlier period we learn that there were at least two types or sizes of quarters on the farms—"the largest kind" and "the smaller ones or cabins." The cabins, also termed "huts" by General Washington, were built by the Negroes themselves of logs daubed with clay. These cabins would have had earthen floors. The larger quarters may have been double cabins, sharing a central chimney, or they may have been

60

single units used communally. While these habitations were primitive, they should be judged by contemporary standards—more miserable perhaps than the peasant cottages of England and the Continent at that period, no worse than the hovels of the Irish peasants, as good as some of the pioneer habitations of the New World. A half century after Niemcewicz wrote his description of the Mount Vernon habitations, Charles Dickens noted that lodgings for the pigs were "nearly as good as many of the human quarters" he observed in western Pennsylvania.

The stockkeeper, or storekeeper, was an important member of the Home House staff. He was charged with the safekeeping and issuance of a wide range of tools and materials, all of which were susceptible to pilferage by the Mount Vernon people for ready resale to unscrupulous buyers in Alexandria. It was essential that the stockkeeper be both honest and alert and that his storeroom be well secured. Most of the items in stock at the outset of the war had been imported from the mother country. This source of supply was now cut off, and ports were blockaded by British men-of-war to prevent the ex-colonists from trading with other markets. The supplies on hand had to be doled out with more than ordinary discrimination. Harness could be repaired, the fittings reused, but there was no certainty of replacement for nails and other small hardware, for carpenter's tools; spades, and scythes for the field hands; oil and pigment for the painters; and twine for the making and repair of nets and seines. Gunpowder was in short supply. Salt, an imported commodity also in custody of the stockkeeper, was soon to be unobtainable.

The stockkeeper was also responsible for the stock of rum on hand, usually a considerable quantity. It was doled out by order of the manager as a stimulant to the mowers in the harvest field, to the men hauling seine in the spring when shad and herring were running, or on any other occasion that required sustained effort. Some of the indentured servants were entitled to a specified rum ration by the terms of their indentures. Rum was dispensed for its narcotic effect by the Mount Vernon midwife to women in childbed; it was truly an all-purpose beverage. George Washington was convinced that its use in moderation contributed to the health and general well-being of his people at Mount Vernon and his troops in the field. He tried to insure a proper supply for both.

The seven laborers listed at the Home House functioned as a special work force, to be employed in the field at harvest time, at the fishery in season, and in filling the ice house at another season. They cut firewood and kept the millrace in repair. These laborers are sometimes referred to in the work accounts as the "ditchers." The ditch banks which they raised made field and boundary fences more effective. Double ditch banks bordered the principal roads within the Mount Vernon boundaries, at the same time draining, defining, and making the roads more serviceable. Within the present boundaries of Mount Vernon, sections of these ditches and banks have escaped obliteration by the bulldozers of the developers who since World War II have subdivided the areas that once comprised the Mount Vernon out-farms.

George Washington's attitude toward slavery is clearly revealed in his writings. It is apparent that the war years widened his horizons and matured his thinking, confirming his sense of the moral wrong and the economic weaknesses of the institution. There is evidence of this enlarged view in his statement of 9 September 1786, to John Francis Mercer: "I never mean (unless some Particular circumstance should compel me to it) to possess another slave by purchase; it being among my first wishes to see some plan adopted, by which slavery in this country may be abolished by slow, sure, and imperceptible degrees."

His own dilemma as a slaveowner became more acute with the passage of time. By natural increase the Mount Vernon slave population grew as his need for workers was reduced by the changeover from planting to field cropping. He was as reluctant to sell slaves as he was to buy. "I am principled against this kind of traffic in the human species," he wrote to a nephew in the last year of his life. By the terms of his will his slaves were granted their freedom upon the death of Mrs.

Washington. His executors were charged with responsibility for the care of the old and the disabled.

However commendable the master's principles in the matter of slavery, there remained the practical problem of compelling a reluctant and improvident people to support themselves with the tools at hand. This stern and realistic aspect of the relationship is reflected in his instructions to his overseers: "I do therefore in explicit terms enjoin it upon you to remain constantly at home (unless called off by unavoidable business or to attend Divine Worship) and to be constantly with your people when there. There is no other sure way of getting work well done and quietly by Negroes; for when an Overlooker's back is turned the most of them will slight their work or be idle altogether" (14 July 1793).

By the standards of a more enlightened and affluent age the situation of the Mount Vernon Negro was grim, but in 1775—with a military conflict threatening death, destruction, and disruption of the economic life of the country—there was a certain built-in security for the Mount Vernon community. It was nearly self-supporting and could be made more so. The Negroes had reasonable assurance of food, clothing, and shelter. Humanitarian and material considerations would assure them also of the continuation of the best medical care available.

REPAIRS AND ALTERATIONS

In addition to the normal activities of the farm, the domestic industries, and the business management of the place, Lund Washington was confronted with a program of major structural developments and landscaping that was scarcely beyond the initial stage when George Washington departed. The plan was an ambitious one, no doubt carefully studied and clearly outlined in the mind of the planner, but Lund's uncertainty about many aspects of the work indicates that it had not been confided to him in detail. The program had been initiated in 1773. In the autumn of that year George Washington sent to his London agent an order for window glass, paint, and hardware, stating that he was "under a necessity of making some repairs to, and alterations in" his house. He gave no hint of the full scope of his plans; perhaps the agent would have feared for his customer's solvency had he been accorded full confidence. At the same time the services of Going Lanphire, master builder, of Loudon County, were engaged. Lanphire's list of framing, plank, hardware, and other materials needed for the additions to the mansion house and a related letter are in the Washington Papers at the Library of Congress.

A program of this scope required time-consuming preparations. Imported materials could scarcely be expected in less than six months from the date of order—twice as long if a letter went astray or a ship was lost.

Oyster shells for lime must be bought, to be barged up the river and burned in a kiln at the river's edge near the mansion. Sand of proper quality was also barged from the bay area to be mixed with the lime for mortar and plaster. Brick were molded on the place, from local clay, and burned in charcoal-fired kilns, close beside the clay pits. The charcoal was produced locally from Mount Vernon wood. Framing came from the forested areas that comprised a large proportion of the Mount Vernon acreage. "Stocks," twelve by twelve inches in cross section, were hewn from large straight-stemmed oaks, to be cut by sawyers into the various dimensions required for sills, beams, posts, joists, and roof rafters. Of necessity this hewing and sawing was done before the timber had seasoned—and hardened. Close inspection of the Mount Vernon Mansion reveals that some frame sections were put together while the members were still green. In place and under stress, they warped as they seasoned, with the result that floors sagged.

That this preliminary processing and gathering together of materials was well in hand a year before the master's departure to attend the Second Continental Congress is indicated by his diary entry of 25 April 1774: "Mr. Lanphire came to work." A note on progress and evidence of the owner's active furtherance of the work appears in his letter of 4 July 1774 to his neighbor, Bryan Fairfax, "I am very much engaged in raising one of the additions to my house, which I think (perhaps it is fancy) goes on better whilst I am present, than in my absence from the workmen." This addition, at the south, or downriver end, would provide a library or study for the master and a master's bedroom above, with a private stairway between, a welcome amenity in a house much frequented by friends, family, and many less welcome guests who presumed upon the traditional Virginia hospitality of the period. When George Washington set forth for Philadelphia ten months later, this first addition was still unfinished.

George Washington's plan for the enlargement of his modest dwelling was so sweeping that its development would practically efface all evidence of the earlier house. The picture of this pre-Revolutionary Mount Vernon is incomplete. Scattered references and archeological findings reveal that there was a central approach to the front door from a gate located at a point now well within the confines of the bowling green. The gardens were smaller, the service lanes did not exist, and an earlier stable on the site of the present structure was of wood. Beneath the grass plots between the mansion colonnades and the courtyard driveway are the sandstone foundations of two small buildings that flanked the main house of the pre-Revolutionary era. In George Washington's diary notation of 27 March 1760, there is a clue to the identity of these small buildings and an indication that there were two companion structures in corresponding relationship to the main house. The entry reads "Agreed to give Mr. William Triplet £18 to build the two houses in the Front of my House (plastering them also), and running Pallisades to them from the Great House and from the Great House to the Wash House and Kitchen also." This diary notation and the two surviving foundations indicate that the smaller house of the earlier period had four principal dependencies, symmetrically placed. The connecting "Pallisades" would have been ornamental fences. The foundations of the dependencies at the other corners cannot be offered in evidence; they would have been obliterated when the lawn was terraced about the new piazza. These clues to the appearance of Mount Vernon at the time of George Washington's departure in May 1775, although they afford but an incomplete picture, are of some interest, for this modest villa was to undergo a transition during his absence and would appear on his return much as the present-day visitor sees it.

OF THINGS MONETARY

In the general's absence Lund was confronted with a diversity of problems, major and minor, and he confided them at length in his weekly letters to his employer. Most of them were, directly or indirectly, monetary. "I would that you should owe no man," he wrote in November. "John Lowe says you owe him 7s. 6d. for a false tail for your hair. If I thought you owed it, I would pay it. I told him you would have paid such a wretch as him upon receiving the tail." George Washington wore his hair long in the manner of the times, powdered and tied in a queue. As Lund's comment here indicates, the queue was supplemented. The commonly held belief that Washington wore a wig is a misconception fostered by Gilbert Stuart's stylized portraits of the presidential period.

"But enough of this," Lund continued. "In money matters, as in all other things, I will do the best I can." There were larger claims, and in the aggregate they exceeded Lund's ability to pay. Gilbert Simpson was building a gristmill for George Washington on the bank of the Youghiogheny River in western Pennsylvania; his expenses must be paid. The mill was nearing completion and should be made to produce revenue as soon as possible, but an indispensable bolting cloth must first be found, purchased, and sent over the mountain. A party of men, sent out in March 1775 to improve lands granted to George Washington in the Ohio Valley, had retreated under threat of Indian hostilities. The value of their improvements had not been properly appraised and recorded to complete the grantee's title, abandoned crops were lost, and buildings would scarcely survive, but returning workmen must be paid.

The current media of exchange imposed complications. The colonies had long been plagued by a shortage of currency and hampered in their trade with the mother country and among themselves by differentials existing between the various media. Tobacco was legal tender in Virginia, and sterling was a common denominator for all of the diverse colonial currencies. But money was never abundant, and the colonists were driven to the use of drafts on their debtors in meeting their obligations. A draft, of course, was no better than the man on whom it was drawn, and they were often protested by the draftee after having passed from hand to hand in a series of financial transactions. The problem of currency and coinage is reflected in the following record of cash left with Lund by Mrs. Washington when she set out for Cambridge:

	£	s	d
Silver Dollars 500 at 6/	150	0	0
Pennsylvania paper	4	10	0
Maryland paper — 6 Dol at 6/	1	16	0
Old Virginia paper much wore	4	0	9
Pistaren's	11	10	0
Half Crowns 5		12	6
Other silver		19	10
Bits 300	9	7	6
Doubloons 9 at 4.8.0	39	12	0
Gold by Weight not know^g the Coins	35	13	9
Half joe 48 / 6 Dollar 36/	4	4	0

To this diverse assortment of minted and printed monies the Congress had recently added its own legal tender, and the depreciation of this "Continental" currency would soon lead to a condition even more chaotic. Gold was the only fully acceptable medium, and as "bad money drives out good," it disappeared from circulation. Lund might turn to his employer for guidance, but no advice could have eased his dilemma materially, or forestalled the greater evils impending.

"THE PEOPLE SHALL BE CLOTHED"

In his letter of 20 August 1775 to Lund, General Washington recommended that "spinning should go forward with all possible dispatch." This was prudent advice, and Lund should have been in a favorable position to carry it out. During the years before the war the textile industry had been developed to a high state at Mount Vernon. Nicholas Cresswell, the young Englishman previously cited, says in his journal that George Washington was noted for having brought "his various manufactories of Linen and Woolen to greater perfection than any man in the Colony." This preeminent position is translated into terms of production by General Washington's own memorandum that records an annual average of sixteen hundred yards of cloth woven over the four-year period 1767–70.

Lund's reports on the subject of spinning were at first discouraging, indicating that the textile industry had declined at Mount Vernon after 1770. The spinning wheels were out of order, workmen were not available to repair them, and new wheels were not to be had. Later Lund was more optimistic: "the people shall be clothed." Each male would be assured of his standard allotment of jacket, breeches, shirts, and stockings. Each woman would have her petticoat, jacket, shifts, and stockings. In January 1776, Lund reported that he had "set a parcel of little people to spinning," and in February, with nine or more wheels spinning, he estimated that these "auckward and young" spinners had spun enough thread to make three hundred yards of linen. Part, if not all, of this linen thread was spun from flax grown on the place. The crop had been introduced in 1765, and diary entries note an expanding planting program for several years thereafter. Wool was also homegrown; 316 sheep were sheared in the spring of 1776. There is no continuous record of spinning, weaving, and tailoring during the war, nor are there production figures that can be accepted as complete for any wartime period. Cash credits to the weaver specify yardage woven, but the continuity of this and other records is broken by a mutilation of Lund's account book; eighteen consecutive pages have been torn out. There is a measure of Lund's achievement in the surviving record for 1778; credits to a journeyman weaver for that year account for over two thousand yards of cloth. More may have been woven by servants, to whom no monetary credits would have been allowed. Although the record is fragmentary, it affords assurance that Lund's resolution was kept. The people were clothed by a home industry completely integrated, from the flax field and the meadow where the sheep grazed to the finished garments from the tailor's bench.

WAR CLOUDS

During the summer and autumn of 1775 Lund's activities were not solely confined to the sphere of his Mount Vernon stewardship. He shared the political sentiments of his employer, and subject only to the limitations of his position, his energies were at the service of the cause. Events in Virginia were rapidly shaping to a situation in which his loyalty to his employer and to the cause would find a common outlet. While General Washington's army was immobilized before Boston, war came to Tidewater Virginia. Even before George Washington's departure from Virginia, Lord Dunmore, the royal governor, had taken the ominous step of removing the colony's reserve of powder from the magazine at Williamsburg to a British warship in the York River. In the tense situation which resulted, a clash between British marines and local militia had been narrowly averted. Early in June 1775, Dunmore followed the powder to the security of a man-of-war. A few weeks later the Assembly, which refused to do business with a governor thus situated, dissolved itself, putting an end to crown government in Virginia.

Dunmore was an impetuous and vindictive character, and the menace of the men-of-war at his disposal was immediately recognized. In July the members of the late Assembly, self-constituted as "the Convention," met in Richmond to organize a provisional government. "Minute Batallions" were decreed in each county, to be drawn from the militia, and martial law was proclaimed in the lower Tidewater area.

Although Dunmore at first confined his maneuvers to the coastline between Yorktown and Norfolk and hostilities there did not commence until October, all Tidewater Virginia was apprehensive. In August, George Washington, writing from Cambridge, asked Lund to thank the gentlemen of Alexandria for their offer of sanctuary, but expressed doubt that Dunmore would "act so low and unmanly a part as to think of seizing Mrs. Washington, by way of revenge upon me." In mid-October 1775, the mistress of Mount Vernon set out with her son and daughter-in-law to visit her sister and brother-in-law, Colonel and Mrs. Bassett, in New Kent County near Williamsburg. There she would be more secure than on the bank of the Potomac. At Lund's request she packed the general's papers and other valuable possessions of small size in trunks before leaving.

On 29 October Lund acknowledged the general's suggestion that navigation on the Potomac be obstructed by sinking ships in the channel at some point as far down the river as possible. He immediately conveyed the suggestion to George Mason of Gunston Hall and other local leaders, but after surveys and prolonged consultation it was agreed that the channel was everywhere too wide or too deep. A battery was proposed, but nothing was done.

In this same letter of 29 October, Lund remarked, "From the accounts I get from you, and what we are daily hearing here, it looks like lost labor to keep on with our building, for should they get burned it will be provoking; but I shall keep on until I am directed to the contrary by you." He was concerned about George Mason's health: "Colonel Mason has been sick ever since he came from the Convention. He looks very badly and he is quite worn out in appearance. He seems to be much disturbed that he is not able to attend the Committee of Safety. I wish he was well; we want him much and shall miss him if it pleases God to take him out of this world." His last paragraph breathed defiance: "I think fifty men well armed might prevent two hundred from burning Mount Vernon, situated as it is; no way to get to it but up a hill, and if I remember right General Gates told me it could not be done by the shipping. I wish I had the muskets I would endeavor to find the men, black or white, that would at least make them pay dear for the attempt."

On 7 November 1775, Dunmore issued his infamous proclamation, declaring martial law throughout the colony, calling upon all persons capable of bearing arms to resort to his standard or to be deemed guilty of treason, and offering freedom to all slaves and indentured servants "appertaining to rebels," who would join his troops. Here indeed was an ultimatum; hope of conciliation was gone. A few Virginians responded to Dunmore's summons. For the great majority there could be no recourse but to arms. That majority was so well organized, so alert at the local level through the committees of safety, that a small minority of loyalists was silenced and rendered ineffective. Virginia was spared the partisan warfare that characterized the Revolutionary struggle in the Carolinas.

Mrs. Washington was still visiting in New Kent County when General Washington's letter inviting her to join him in Cambridge reached Mount Vernon. Lund forwarded it by special messenger. She turned homeward a few days later and made preparations for the long, arduous journey. Of this brief period Lund noted in his letter of 14 November to his employer, "This house has been so crowded with company since Mrs. Washington came home, that I fear many things are left undone that should have been done before she left home. I write in haste and a little confused."

Mrs. Washington left Mount Vernon about the middle of

November, accompanied by her son John Parke Custis and his wife. The young couple continued with her to headquarters and remained through the winter. On behalf of the Fairfax Committee Custis carried with him £53.13.3 to be distributed at his stepfather's discretion "among the deserving poor of Boston." More was promised by the committee as additional monies were received. In an accompanying letter over the signatures of John Dalton and William Ramsay, surprise was expressed that the committee in Boston had never acknowledged 162 barrels of flour, 50 bushels of beans, and 11 barrels of bread that had been shipped in November 1774, at a cost to the Fairfax Committee of £268.13.19, with shipping charges. Mrs. Washington was also accompanied by George Lewis—a son of the general's sister Betty and her husband, Fielding Lewis of Fredericksburg. Young Lewis was bound for headquarters to offer his services as a military aide to his uncle.

In a letter to the general by the hand of his son, Fielding Lewis reported that commercial activities in Virginia were pretty much at a standstill. "I do not find that any money is paid to anybody. I do not receive a shilling." Lewis had accepted the management of a local gun manufactory, a public-spirited activity on his part that would impoverish him. In his letter he predicted that by the first of the year the fifty men then employed would be turning out about twelve complete guns a day. They were also making locks to replace those that Dunmore had removed from the guns in the powder magazine at Williamsburg. While thus vigorously preparing for war, Lewis still hoped that there would be an accomodation. Without the American trade, he predicted, "Great Britain must fall."

Mrs. Washington and her companions stopped in Philadelphia for several days. Her arrival in the colonial metropolis was reported in the Pennsylvania *Gazette* of 22 November, as was her departure a week later. To a young friend in Alexandria the general's lady wrote, "I don't doubt but you have seen the Figuer our arrival made in the Philadelphia paper and I left it in as great pomp as if I had been a great somebody." From headquarters the general dispatched Lt. Col. George Baylor, a dashing Virginia cavalryman, with fresh horses to meet the party and to provide escort on the last leg of the journey. In the letter to her young friend in Alexandria Mrs. Washington reported that New England was beautiful and the journey pleasant; they found the general well and "came within the month to Camp." For a Virginia matron in her early forties who had never before been north of Alexandria, this journey was a brave venture.

Lund was relieved of responsibility for Mrs. Washington's safety, but thought in any case by this time that Dunmore would now postpone coming or sending up the river until spring. Perhaps this was more a pious hope than a belief; in the same letter of 14 November he wrote, "I believe we must defend our plantations upon the Potomac with our muskets. I believe the gentlemen are ready and willing to turn out and defend any mans property, but the common people are most hellishly frightened."

On 3 December 1775, Lund wrote:

Our Dunmore has at length published his much dreaded proclamation, declaring freedom to all indented servants and slaves (the property of rebels) that will repair to his majesty's standard, being able to bear arms. What effect it will have upon those sort of people, I cannot tell. I think if there was no white servants in this family I should be under no apprehension about the slaves. However I am determined that if any of them create any confusion, to make an example of him. Sears who is at work here, says there is not a man of them, but would leave us if they believed they could make their escape, Tom Spears excepted. And yet through having no fault to find,—liberty is sweet.

In January he reported that the servants behaved "as well as common" and that he had no misgivings concerning the Negroes. There is no indication that Dunmore's proclamation caused any defections or serious unrest at Mount Vernon.

Lund Washington might be excused had he referred to "our Dunmore" in less restrained language. Not content with promoting civil war and insurrection in the more settled parts of the colony, the deposed royal governor had concocted a plan with one John Connelly to organize the Indians and "disaffected" persons of the Ohio Valley. Connelly, an able man who was well acquainted with the frontier, had journeyed to Boston, where the plan had been approved by General Gage, and returned to Dunmore's headquarters unmolested. Fortunately, General Washington had received a warning letter and sent it posthaste to Lund for transmittal to George Mason. Local committees of safety on both sides of the Potomac were alerted, and late in November Connelly was intercepted near Hagerstown en route to Fort Pitt. Papers in his possession revealed that he was to have marched eastward in the spring with a force of loyalists and Indians, joining Dunmore's fleet and auxiliaries at Alexandria on 20 April 1776. Connelly's arrest put an end to this sinister threat.

Lund's December letters to his employer describe a wintry scene and reflect a melancholy state of mind. The weather was cold; the river was blocked with ice. He would prepare to move the household furniture in the spring, but there was so much else to be considered. Food was of more immediate importance than furniture. The cornhouses were too close to the river shore, certain to be burned if Dunmore's threat materialized. There was no adequate transport for bulky commodities, no safe place of storage, no local market. He considered shipping a cargo of flour and corn to some neutral port, to be exchanged for arms and ammunition: a most profitable transaction if it could be. effected. Lund thought the risks were not greater in shipping than in leaving the corn and flour where they were, "but as you have hitherto been unlucky in trade and I have often heard you say you would not venture again, I have declined it, though I think it would be best to do it."

The shortage of salt throughout Virginia was so acute at this time as to create a condition of near panic in some areas, which necessitated local rationing of such meager supplies as could be obtained. With ports blockaded by British warships, the shortage continued. Cresswell relates that in December 1776, a mob of forty Dutchmen from the Piedmont area descended upon Alexandria, armed with swords and clubs, intending to obtain salt by violence if other means failed. They were appeased by an allotment of three pints each. Salt meat was a principal element in the diet of the population generally; in the Tidewater area it was supplemented by salt fish. Cresswell thought salt so important that the people would revolt if denied it, but this was probably the wishful thinking of a loyalist. Lund was the fortunate custodian of a considerable reserve supply of salt. In February 1776, he reported that he had put 300 bushels in fish barrels for removal to the barn at Muddy Hole, where it would be less exposed to waterborne raiders.

Rum was another important staple of which Lund held a good supply—over a thousand gallons. Such a large stock posed a problem. There was always a danger of pilferage, and in time of turmoil there were more serious potentialities. Lund thought it prudent to sell most of this rum and had little difficulty in finding a market for it in the neighborhood.

On 1 January 1776, British sailors and marines fired the Norfolk waterfront. On 17 January Lund reported that "the Alexandrians expect to have their town burned by the enemy soon. They do not take any steps to prevent it. They put their trust in the Convention, and the Convention, I believe, in God—for I cannot learn what they are about." The Minute Battalion marched off to Williamsburg, taking with them nearly all the serviceable guns in the country. "Our militia exercises with clubs," Lund wrote, "if they come to close quarters in an engagement they perhaps may do some execution, but not otherwise."

Lund's weekly letters are written in a rambling style with little attention to paragraphing or organization of subject matter. For this reason they are seldom adapted to lengthy quotation, but in his letter of 31 January he follows one train of thought through several pages with unwonted unity, and what he reports is best told in his own words:

Alexandria is much alarmed and indeed the whole neighborhood. A report prevails that there are five large ships laying off the mouth of Cone [Coan Creek, near the mouth of the Potomac]. An express from County to County brings the information, although the River is blocked with ice. The women and children are leaving Alexandria and stowing themselves into every little hut they can get, out of reach of the enemies cannon as they think, every wagon, cart, and pack horse that can be got, are employed in moving the goods out of town. The militia are all up (but not in arms) for indeed they have none or at least very few. I expect the five large ships will prove to be five oyster boats. I could wish if we are to have our neighborhood invaded soon, they would first send a tender or two among us. I want much to see how the people would behave upon the occasion. I proposed to the inhabitants of Alexandria that they should (before this alarm came) throw up an intrenchment from the mouth of Hunting Creek up to the upper end of the town or indeed farther, assuring them that in my opinion they might by so doing prevent them from landing and consequently from burning the town, unless they should be provided with a bomb vessel, and I believe as yet they have none in this colony, for they threw none in Norfolk. But their answer was what can we do. We have wrote to the Convention, giving them a statement of our incapacity for defense and praying that something may be done for the preservation of this town. But they say they are determined to fight although they move out their effects. I believe they will. I am about packing up your china, glass, etc. into barrels and shall continue to pack into casks, whatever I think should be put up in that way, and other things into chests, trunks, bundles, etc., and then I shall be able at the shortest notice to move your things out of harms way (at least for a while). some to Mrs. Barnes and the rest into Morrises barn; and if they are found not to be safe there, move them further after. I fear the destruction will be great although the greatest care be taken. Mr. McCarthy has offered me his cellar to put your wine, rum, etc. in. I shall either send it there or to Mrs. Barnes. She tells me she has reserved one room in her cellar, and one room up stairs for me. I have engaged two hogsheads of rum in Port Tobacco, which will be delivered so soon as the River will permit, at 5/ gallon. The rest I suppose I shall be obliged to move. As yet I have moved nothing but your papers. Everybody I see tells me if they could have notice they would immediately come and defend your property, so long as they had life. From Loudon, Prince William, Fauquier and this county one hundred men, in my opinion, could prevent one thousand from landing here to do mischief. William Stevens, so soon as the alarm got to the neighborhood of Bladensburg, went to Georgetown, crossed upon the ice and came here, he says to fight in defense of your property. . . . The bacon when it is sufficiently smoked, I think to have put up in casks with ashes and if necessary move it, together with some pork which I have already put up into Barrels. These are dreadful times to give people so much trouble and vexation. Fighting and being killed is the least troublesome part.

In a postscript to this same letter Lund dissents from the prevailing state of alarm. He will move the furniture to a place of safety if the general thinks best, but in his own opinion the troops now with Dunmore, unless they should be reinforced, are "too trifling to think of taking and fortifying Alexandria."

In the last two letters of this, the longest surviving sequence to George Washington, 29 February and 7 March 1776, Lund reported that he had many things packed and would move them. Locally, there were encouraging signs of preparation for defensive action. Cannons were being brought from Winchester and other places. Vessels were being built in Alexandria, and a regiment had been stationed in the little town of Dumfries, fifteen miles below Mount Vernon. The vessels referred to by Lund were two "row-gallies," which had been authorized by the Committee of Safety for the protection of the Potomac River. On 2 April George Mason wrote to General Washington that the galleys were well advanced in construction and that three sloops were being armed. These boats, it was hoped, would be effective against the enemy's small craft, and their shallow draft would afford safe haven in creeks where larger warships could not venture.

Dunmore's forces did not ascend the Potomac until July, when a fleet of three men-of-war, an armed ship, and several small auxiliaries reached the mouth of Aquia Creek, on the Virginia side of the river twenty-five miles below Mount Vernon. The home of William Brent, a little above the mouth of the creek, was burned. John Parke Custis's account of this foray in an August letter to his stepfather reflects no credit on one unit of the Virginia militia. He wrote:

You have no doubt heard of the men-of-war coming up Potow-
mack as far as Mr. Brent's, whose house they burnt with several
outhouses and some stacks of wheat. A Captain James with sixty
militia were stationed there who all got drunk, and kept challenging
the men-of-war to come ashore, and upbraiding them with cowardice. Hammond sent one hundred and fifty men, who landed about
ten o'clock under cover of a gondola and tender. The militia were
asleep after their drinking frolic, and did not discover the enemy
until they landed and their vessels began to fire. Captain James
desired his men to shift for themselves, and ran off without firing
a gun. A young man by name of Combs stayed until he killed three
of the enemy. Colonel Grayson appearing with thirty Prince William volunteers, the enemy thought proper to retire to their ships.
Captain James is to be tried for cowardice. The fleet, after performing this exploit, returned down the river to George's island, from
whence they have been drove off by Major Price with some loss.
They are gone down the bay in a most sickly condition. I have not
heard where they have stopped. Before they left the island they
burned several vessels, and I hear that two sloops belonging to
them have fallen into Captain Boucher's hands.

Young Custis's account of the sorry behavior of the local
militia at Brent's would have been all too readily understood
by the general in the light of his own current experience with
their New England counterparts, who, in his words, "come
in you cannot tell how, go, you cannot tell when; and act you
cannot tell where; consume your Provisions, exhaust your
Stores, and leave you at last in a critical moment." By the end
of the war he might have added that at the most critical moment, when confronted by a unit of British regulars in line of
battle, they were likely to leave with great celerity, having on
more than one occasion established unenviable records for
sustained flight.

Dunmore could harass and destroy along the immediate
shore of the bay and its tributaries, but he could not reestab-
lish his authority beyond the range of his ship's guns. His
measures, political and military, had only stiffened the spirit
of resistance. Early in August 1776, he quitted the waters of
the state, dispersed his forces, and joined the British fleet off

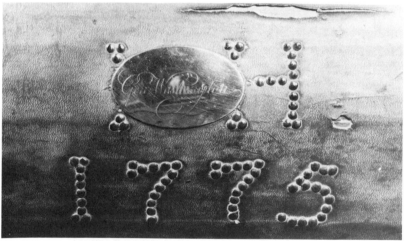

LEATHER TRUNK

Fig. 12. This memento of General Washington's military service is recorded in a bill among his papers at the Library of Congress as a "Travelling hair trunk." The initials beneath his own name plate (*inset view*) are those of Joseph Head, who received £2/16/0 for the trunk. The bill is dated 4 April 1776, the day the general commenced his southward journey from Boston to New York, where he would once again confront his seaborne adversaries.
(Courtesy of the Mount Vernon Ladies' Association.)

79

New York. At the end of the year he returned to England, and Virginia saw him no more.

MARTHA WASHINGTON TAKES THE SMALLPOX

In April of 1776, after the British evacuation of Boston, General Washington moved southward; Mrs. Washington followed with her son and daughter-in-law. They were delayed en route by Jackie's illness, but joined the general at his New York headquarters on 17 April. The young couple went on to Mount Airy, the home of Nelly's father, Benedict Calvert, in Prince Georges County, Maryland, a few miles east of Mount Vernon, where their second child, Elizabeth, was born in August. A first child had died in infancy a year earlier.

In May Mrs. Washington journeyed on to Philadelphia to undergo inoculation for smallpox, a measure of which her husband was a strong advocate, for his family and for his troops. "The propriety of it is so striking that it cannot admit of a doubt," he wrote. In time of war an epidemic of smallpox, so easily communicable, could be more devastating than a hostile army. George Washington, of course, was immune to the disease, having survived it at the age of nineteen in Barbados, where he had gone with his elder brother Lawrence in the vain hope of a cure for the latter's consumption.

Inoculation was an ordeal that Mrs. Washington had long dreaded and evaded, but the time had come. Although there is no surviving evidence of an ultimatum on the part of her husband, it is strongly inferential that Mrs. Washington found herself under necessity of being inoculated if she wished to join the general in winter quarters another time. Inoculation with infectious "matter" from a convalescing patient induced a mild attack of smallpox. This protective measure had been introduced into the colonies as early as 1720. When properly employed it was safe and effective, but ignorance and carelessness occasionally resulted in mortality, and

Fig. 13a. Martha Washington (1731–1802)

Fig. 13b. John Park Custis (1754–81)

MR. PEALE'S MINIATURES

Fig. 13. On 19 August 1776, Charles Willson Peale noted in his diary that he received twenty-eight dollars from Mrs. Washington for her likeness in miniature. The portrait was probably executed during her second sojourn in Philadelphia that summer, rather than during the first, when she was under inoculation. The miniature of her son, Jackie, is thought to have been painted by Peale after the young man's death in 1781, based on his 1772 miniature of Custis. This double miniature remained in the family for five generations before finding its way back to Mount Vernon. *(Courtesy of the Mount Vernon Ladies' Association.)*

there was a widespread prejudice against the practice. On 4 June General Washington was able to report to his brother-in-law, Burwell Bassett, from Philadelphia—where he was in conference with the congress—that Mrs. Washington was "now in the Small Pox by Innoculation and like to have it very favourably having got through the Fever and not more than about a dozen Pustules appearing (this being the 13th day since the Infection was received)."

From Mount Airy young Custis (whose own inoculation had been carefully effected without the preknowledge of his oversolicitous mother) acknowledged the news of his mother's progress in a letter of 10 June to his stepfather: "I do with the most filial Affection congratulate you both on this Happy Event, as She can now attend you to any Part of the Continent with pleasure, unsullied by the Apprehensions of that Disorder; and whose presence will alleviate the Care and Anxiety which public Transactions may occasion, this Consideration has added much to the pleasure I feel on this Occasion, as your Happiness when together will be much greater than when you are apart." (See fig. 13.)

To Bassett General Washington had stated that Mrs. Washington might return to New York following her convalescence, "if matters there are in such a situation as to make it a fit place for her to remain." The general's lady did return to New York when she had regained her strength, turning southward again in early July when the arrival of Howe's Fleet in the bay and his landing on Staten Island indicated that New York was no longer to be "a fit place for her." As Mount Vernon was not a secure haven either so long as the shores of Chesapeake Bay and its tributaries were at the mercy of Dunmore's vessels, Mrs. Washington lingered in Philadelphia. Her departure from that city can be dated about 20 September, as it is recorded that she stopped in Baltimore overnight on 23 September. She was accompanied by Thomas Nelson, Jr., member of Congress from Virginia, and by Mrs. Nelson, John Parke Custis, George Lewis, Nathanial Nelson, and Robert Gates, all of whom would go their separate ways south of the Potomac, with the exception of Custis—who had been urged, with his wife, to make Mount Vernon their home for the duration.

With or without her son and daughter-in-law there could be no peace for Martha Washington in her lonely isolation. She had qualified by the ordeal of inoculation to join her husband another time, but she may well have wondered whether there would be another winter encampment. News, good or bad, would be long on the road, and it was more likely to be bad than good. She knew what the world had yet to learn—that her husband was inflexibly determined to hazard his life and reputation in carrying out the commission he had received from the Congress. He might remonstrate against what he thought to be unwise policies, but he would faithfully comply with the Congress's decisions. Martha Washington knew of his fear that the poorly disciplined, ill-armed militia would not stand up against British regulars. It is possible that she had heard before leaving Philadelphia of the disgraceful incident at Kip's Bay. Here the general's worst fears had been realized as the militia fled in wild disorder before a small advancing force of British and Hessians. Arriving at a critical moment with an escort of a few young officers, he had tried to rally the fleeing troops. According to Tench Tilghman he had ridden among them exhorting and, in his wrathful despair, caning their officers, but to no avail. He and his escort found themselves abandoned within close range of the advancing enemy. A well-timed volley could have struck them down. Martha Washington may not yet have learned of this sorry incident, but she could have predicted her husband's conduct in such a circumstance. (See fig. 14.) Her knowledge of his courage and his temper did not lessen her anxiety. She knew that George Washington had no hope of accommodation with the mother country, no expectation of clemency as a defeated rebel general. She certainly knew of his intention to seek asylum on his western lands if worse came to worst. At Mount Vernon in the autumn of 1776 Martha Washington had much to ponder.

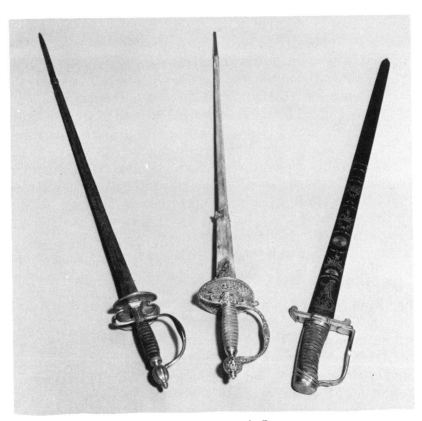

GEORGE WASHINGTON'S SWORDS

Fig. 14. To each of five nephews—William Augustine Washington, George Lewis, George Steptoe Washington, Bushrod Washington, and Samuel Washington—the general bequeathed a sword, with the injunction that they were "not to unsheath them for the purpose of shedding blood, except it be in self defense, or in the defense of their country and its rights; and in the latter case, to keep them unsheathed and prefer falling with them in their hands, to the relinquishment thereof." The first charge laid upon his nephews reflects Washington's strong disapproval of dueling as a means of resolving private quarrels. The second is more significant as an affirmation, in his final testament, of the inflexible resolution with which he accepted his commission as commander-in-chief from the Continental Congress.

Three of the five swords selected by the nephews under their uncle's bequest are in the Mount Vernon collection. The fourth, described as a rapier with a filagreed hilt, was selected for William A. Washington, in his absence, by his cousin Bushrod. This sword is in the New York State

IMPROVEMENTS GO FORWARD

In February of 1776 Lund Washington had written a qualified recommendation to his employer: "I think if you could be of opinion that your buildings would not be destroyed this summer, it would be best to have the other addition to the end of your house raised, the chimney pulled down, and put up again, that being the most troublesome part of the work. But this cannot be done without a master workman, unless you choose once more to try Lanphire." The timbers for this addition had been cut out and were lying exposed to the weather at the north end of the building. They should be framed, raised, and closed in before seasoning and warping rendered them unusable. As Lund's letters to General Washington from 7 March to the end of this year are missing and his account book is of no assistance for the period, the sequel to his recommendation is drawn from references to the addition in two of General Washington's letters to Lund. In the first of these, from New York, 19 August 1776, the general gave detailed directions for the planting of groves at each end of the house; that at the north end to consist of "locusts altogether" and that at the south "of all the

Library at Albany. It was badly damaged when the state capitol burned in 1911. The fifth sword, chosen by Samuel Washington, was presented by his son to the United States Congress in 1843. It is now at the Smithsonian. *Left*: This dress sword, said to have been worn by Washington at funerals, was the choice of Bushrod Washington. It is reported to have been damaged and the scabbard destroyed when it was hidden away during the Civil War. Two inscriptions in Latin, "Do What is Right" and "Fear No Man," were recorded before they were obliterated. *Center*: The sword chosen by George Lewis, another dress sword, is said to have been worn on state occasions. *Right*: The Prussian sword chosen by George Steptoe Washington. It bears the inscription "Destroyer of Despotism, Protector of Freedom, Determined Man, Take from my Son's Hand this Sword, I Pray Thee. Theophilus Alte Solinger." On the reverse it is inscribed to George Washington.
(Courtesy of the Mount Vernon Ladies' Association.)

clever kind of Trees (especially flowering ones) that can be got." The north grove, he cautioned, should not be planted until after the addition at that end had been closed in and the chimney rebuilt. Otherwise the young trees would be "broke down, defaced and spoil'd." He closed with a request that Lanphire be hastened about this addition. In the second letter, from the Heights of Harlem, 30 September, he gave detailed advice about the relation of the new chimney to the existing fireplace openings in the older part of the house.

General Washington's letters to Lund often afford a striking contrast in subject matters. He confided his problems as commander-in-chief, perhaps more freely than to any other correspondent; in the same letter he might give directions and advice about the most minute details of Mount Vernon management. In this letter of 30 September 1776, he wrote: "If men will stand by me (which by the by I despair of), I am resolved not to be forced from this ground while I have life." Such intimate confidences, entrusted to a precarious post, may seem indiscreet, but the significance of this range of letter content lies in its revelation of an abiding interest in life as a private citizen on the bank of the Potomac, his confidence in his kinsman, and his need to be distracted by more agreeable plans and problems than those that so closely beset him.

On the strength of these references in General Washington's letters, it is assumed that Lanphire returned to work and that the north mansion addition was raised and enclosed by the autumn of 1776. Plastering, trimming, and decoration of the large room that constituted the first floor of the north addition and whose high ceiling eliminated a second floor, would be deferred until the master could direct the work himself. (See fig. 15.)

The annals of Mount Vernon are fragmentary and uninformative for the year 1777. General Washington's letters to Lund are missing, and Lund's single surviving letter to his employer, dated 24 December 1777, is brief; it contains no mention of improvements. Lund's account book is the sole source of information on this subject for the period. Entries

THE NEW ROOM, SOUTH ELEVATION

Fig. 15. "The chimney in the new room should be exactly in the middle of it—doors and everything else to be exactly answerable and uniform—in short I would have the whole executed in a masterly manner." George Washington to Lund Washington from Colonel Morris's on the Heights of Harlem, 30 September 1776.
(Courtesy of the Mount Vernon Ladies' Association.)

reveal that Lanphire and two of his men were active. The inference is that the piazza was erected in 1777, the sole evidence being a brief debit to cash for "3 Barrels of Tar for Pitchg the Piazza." James Hogan is credited with making 100,000 brick, 1700 large tile, and 1250 smaller. On the basis of the cash entry the evidence for the erection of the piazza seems definite enough that some of these brick may be assigned to the footings of the structure and the building of three wine vaults beneath the pavement. The brick tiles may have been intended for the pavement of the piazza. If so, they served only ad interim, as General Washington imported cut stone for this pavement in 1785.

"It is a matter of doubt whether I shall be able to prevail on Lanphire to come to work or not," Lund wrote in the late winter of 1778. A week later he reported, "Lanphire was here some little time past, after some conversations with him I found he had very little thoughts of working here much more. He said money could not purchase the necessaries of life and that he must endeavor to make them. Finding I could have nothing better with him, I told him if he would stick to his work and endeavor to finish it, I would make him a present at shearing time of forty pounds of wool and next Fall thirty barrels of corn. He has promised that he will be here very shortly and stick close to the work, and that nothing but sickness shall take him from it." A month after this hopeful communication, Lund was again uncertain and annoyed:

Of all the worthless men living Lanphire is the greatest, no act or temptation of mine can prevail on him to come to work notwithstanding his repeated promises to do so. I wanted so much to get the windows finished in the pediment that I might have the garret passage plastered and cleaned out before Mrs. Washington's return [from Valley Forge]. Beside this the scaffolding in the front of the house cannot be taken away before it is finished. This prevents me from putting up the steps to the great front door, a work I want Harry Young to be about. I think he will be here today and stick to his work.

The passage last quoted indicates that more than the piazza had been attempted, but not completed, the previous year. Proximity of that more prominent roof structure, the cupola, to the pediment, suggests that it also may have been added in 1777 or 1778. There is no reference to it in the managerial correspondence or accounts for the war years; but as General Washington noted that the cupola leaked during his first winter at home, it seems reasonable to credit it to Lanphire and to assume that it is contemporary with the piazza and the pediment.

When Lund offered Lanphire corn and wool as incentive payments in 1778, he anticipated that the covered ways connecting the mansion with the kitchen and the servants' hall would be completed that year. His three surviving letters for the remainder of the year reveal that Lanphire lacked necessary assistance. In the last of these letters, 2 September, he expressed doubts that the covered ways would be erected. General Washington's letter of 18 December 1778 to Lund reflects the latter's belief that he had made a bad bargain with Lanphire. The general warned, apparently in response to a request for advice, that until the covered ways and other work contemplated in the bargain had been completed, "the corn . . . should be delivered but little at a time, for if he gets the whole at once you may I suppose, catch him as you can."

Lund's account book reveals that Lanphire worked 112 days in 1778, and a single helper 267. Lanphire himself did no more work at Mount Vernon; one of his men worked on through 1779 and received a final payment for his employer on 8 January 1780. Presumably he completed the raising and covering of the colonnades, as contemplated when Lund made new terms with Lanphire in the spring of 1778. Lund's letters to General Washington for the entire period from 2 September 1778 to 15 May 1782 are missing, and the building program is not mentioned in any of General Washington's surviving letters to Lund during this interval. It can only be reported on the authority of Lund's account book that the colonnade passages were paved in 1781 and the ceilings were plastered in 1783.

With Lund's final payment to Lanphire's assistant in January 1780, he disappears from the record; his work at Mount Vernon was ended. Certain finishing touches were yet to be added, but the mansion and its courtyard dependencies had been substantially developed to the forms and relationships in which they now exist.

THE ARCHITECT OF MOUNT VERNON

In *A Brief & True Report Concerning Williamsburg in Virginia* by Rutherfoord Goodwin, (Colonial Williamsburg, 1940), the author writes: "it should be pointed to that the eighteenth Century Buildings of Williamsburg and of its surrounding Countryside were built by a limited Number of Master Builders, Mechanics, Artisans, and their Apprentices, representing but a few Generations in Time and Tradition. Again, these Builders were to a considerable Degree limited by the Implements and Materials which were readily available." This statement holds true for all of Tidewater Virginia, with the observation that as the distance from the capitol increased, so did the difficulty of procuring competent workmen. It could be stated also as a generality that in the more distant and recently settled areas such as the upper reaches of the tidal Potomac, the lesser affuence of the planters usually dictated smaller and less-refined structures. The one-and-one-half story villa that George Washington's father built at Mount Vernon in the mid-1730s might be cited as typical of these more modest structures.

It will be noted that Goodwin's above-quoted statement makes no mention of architects. The omission was not an oversight. Architects in the modern sense of the word did not appear in Virginia or, for that matter, in British America, until quite late in the eighteenth century. They had no part in the design or creation of domestic Virginia structures prior to the Federal period.

If we consult Samuel Johnson's dictionary, we learn that an architect, during the period that concerns us here, was "a professor of the art of building, a builder." Architecture was "the art or science of building." There is no mention of design or designing. By contrast, the modern dictionary defines an architect as "one who practices architecture," and architecture as "the profession of designing buildings." At the earlier period, the builder, of course, consulted his client, just as the tailor consulted his customer, and in each instance, the prevailing fashion and the means of the client largely determined the end product.

At Gunston Hall, the home of George Mason, we find an example of the prevailing relationship between client and builder. William Buckland, master builder, came to Gunston as an indentured servant, following a seven-year apprenticeship with a London joiner. He was four years at Gunston as a carpenter and joiner at an annual wage of £20. At the end of this period his employer certified that Buckland had had entire direction of the carpenters and joiners and that he was a complete master of the carpenters and joiners business "both in theory and practice." Buckland's work at Gunston and later in Annapolis has an important place in our architectural heritage. In present-day terminology we think of him as a distinguished architect, but to his contemporaries he was a master builder.

At Mount Vernon the relationship between employer and builder was the conventional one that existed at Gunston and elsewhere throughout Virginia. At Mount Vernon it is first evident just prior to George Washington's marriage in 1759, when the story-and-a-half house built by his father in the mid-1730s was enlarged to two and one-half stories. (See fig. 16.) John Patterson was the master builder. He was a literate man, as evidenced by his letters to his employer, who was on the frontier in command of the Virginia Regiment. That he was a competent craftsman is manifest in the interior finish of the Mansion central hall, the downstairs bedroom, and the west parlor, which remained unchanged in the final program of enlargement and embellishment of the house. Washington's letters to Patterson have not survived, nor do we have any memoranda or sketches in his hand relating to the work of this period. His business ledger records a payment to Patterson, "By the Amount of your Acct for work on my House, etc. Including charges against me to this date," of £328.0.5, a substantial sum for the time.

Going Lanphire, the other master builder associated with the Mount Vernon structures, did not deserve Lund Washington's characterization as worthless. Lund's own report of

AUGUSTINE WASHINGTON'S HOUSE
c.1735 TO 1757

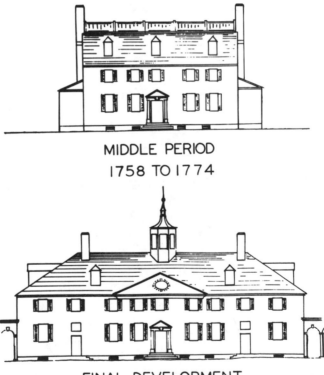

MIDDLE PERIOD
1758 TO 1774

FINAL DEVELOPMENT
1774 TO 1799

EVOLUTION OF THE MANSION

Fig. 16. Conjectural drawings of the mansion by Worth Bailey. *(Courtesy of the Mount Vernon Ladies' Association.)*

TWO ELEVATIONS OF THE MANSION WEST FRONT

Fig. 17a, above: Washington's sketch of the west front of the mansion before 1774, as he proposed to develop it. *Fig. 17b, below:* Measured drawing of the west front showing actual positioning of the windows, pediment, and cupola.
(Courtesy of the Mount Vernon Ladies' Association.)

the man's statement that "money could not purchase the necessities of life," to explain his reluctance to continue the work in hand, is revealing enough. Inflation had made his bargain unrealistic; payment in kind was a practical solution to the problem. Lanphire's preliminary list of framing needed for the enlargement of the mansion and his accompanying letter indicate that he understood the scope of the work. Two hundred years later, the mansion with its colonnades, piazza, and courtyard dependencies endures as an evidence of his mastery of his craft.

The long gaps in the correspondence of the war years between George Washington and Lund deny us knowledge as to the exact extent of the guidance the latter may have had from his absent employer where Lanphire's work was concerned. That there was an overall plan is apparent from the simple line drawing in George Washington's hand of the mansion courtyard elevation and the plan of the basement that has survived. (See figs. 17, 18, 19, and 20.) It should be noted also that Lanphire could have had a great deal of on-the-spot direction and guidance before Washington's departure in the spring of 1775. There may have been, too, other of the master's sketches, no longer extant, simple plans of the piazza, the colonnades, and the outbuildings. Washington's related ground plan of the mansion and other features of the formal area survived long enough to be copied by Benson Lossing at the middle of the nineteenth century. It offers convincing evidence that there was an overall plan and that it was George Washington's own. It is well adapted to the site, and its esthetic virtues are apparent. Functionally also it deserves commendation in the light of the activities and the large supporting population domiciled in the service areas immediately adjoining the mansion, with a minimum of intrusion on the master and his household.

Many elements of the overall plan, some probably unsketched, were incomplete when Washington returned home at the end of the war. The greenhouse and its wings were not to be built until 1785. Planting and landscaping of the formal area was interrupted by the presidency and resumed after his

WEATHER VANE

Fig. 18. While in Philadelphia as one of Virginia's delegates to the Constitutional Convention, George Washington found time to have this biblically inspired weather vane fabricated by Joseph Rakestraw, a local craftsman in metal. The general's directions for its painting and installation survive in his letter of 12 August 1787 to his nephew George Augustine Washington at Mount Vernon. For nearly two centuries this metallic symbol of peace has reported the direction of the wind, while the spire to which it attaches has served as a lightning rod.
(Courtesy of the Mount Vernon Ladies' Association.)

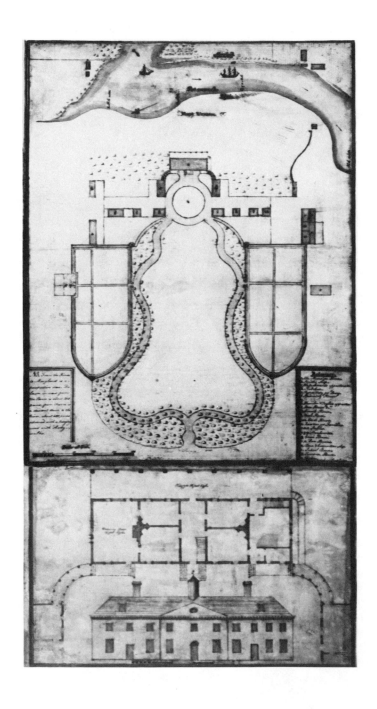

retirement, but time ran out; his plans for the development
and embellishment of Mount Vernon were never fully realized. The day before he died, while suffering from the first
symptoms of his fatal illness, his secretary recorded that he
"went out in the afternoon into the ground between the
House and the River to mark some trees which were to be
cut down in the improvement of that spot."

For over forty years, despite the major diversions created
by his services to his country, George Washington's thoughts
and energies were devoted at every opportunity to the development of his "home house" and the cultivation of its surrounding acres. Although he had the assistance of able crafts-
men and with their collaboration derived design details from
one or another of the numerous English manuals and pattern
books that were dedicated to the use of master builders, the
unifying overall development plan through the years was his
own. His stepgrandson, George Washington Parke Custis, in
his *Recollections and Private Memoirs of Washington*, says, "Washington was his own architect and builder, laying off everything himself. The buildings, gardens, and grounds all rose
to ornament and usefulness under his fostering hand." The
distinguished Polish patriot Niemcewicz, who was a guest at
Mount Vernon after the Revolution, wrote with the critical
discrimination of a traveled European, "The whole plantation, the garden, and the rest prove well that a man born with
natural taste may guess a beauty without having ever seen its
model."

THE VAUGHAN PLAN

Fig. 19. This highly refined ground plan of the mansion, its dependencies,
and the surrounding planted areas, with the attached elevation and floor
plan of the mansion, was sketched by Samuel Vaughan from notes and
dimensions that he recorded on a visit to Mount Vernon during the summer of 1787, while the general was attending the Constitutional Convention in Philadelphia. There are minor discrepancies in the mansion elevation and the delineation of the plantings about the bowling green, but
the overall accuracy of the plan is attested by Washington's letter to
Vaughan acknowledging its receipt.
(Courtesy of the Mount Vernon Ladies' Association.)

THE NEW-ROOM WINDOW AND ITS ENGLISH ANTECEDENT

Fig. 20. The Mount Vernon Palladian window (above) and the sketch in Batty Langley's *Builder's and Workman's Treasury of Design* (London, 1756) from which it derives (on facing page).
(Courtesy of the Mount Vernon Ladies' Association.)

Bryan Fairfax, to whom George Washington had announced the raising of the first addition to his house in 1774, was among the first to see the building in a substantially completed state. On 9 March 1778, he wrote to the general, who was in winter quarters at Valley Forge, "I was yesterday at Mount Vernon, where I hope it will please God to return you in time, and I like the House because it is uncommon for there has always appeared too great a Sameness in our buildings." This is the earliest recorded comment on the Mount Vernon dwelling as its final state of development became recognizable.

In their positioning, the main house, wings, and connecting colonnades are reminiscent of the Governor's Palace at Williamsburg. The proportions of the two main buildings vary, but the overall relationships are quite similar. In each instance the entrance opens to a circular courtyard with a spacious lawn, or "green," beyond. As the Governor's Palace is earlier and was familiar to George Washington, it may well have influenced his overall design. Two other great houses of the period, Mannsfield, home of Mann Page near Fredericksburg, and Mount Airy, home of the Tayloes on the north bank of the Rappahannock opposite Tappahannock, had this same basic plan. Mount Airy still stands, but Mannsfield was destroyed by fire during the Civil War.

The most uncommon architectural feature of George Washington's newly enlarged dwelling was the high-columned piazza that extends the full length of the house on the river side. The detail of the columns seems to derive from one of the English manuals, Langley's *City and Country Builders' Treasury*, but there is no known precedent for the long, covered gallery, or piazza. It was remarked upon by George Washington's guests as an innovation. This piazza commands a majestic view of the Potomac for a distance of several miles in each direction, upriver and downriver. The near shore is only a few hundred feet from the piazza. The bluff on which the house stands has a commanding elevation, and the wide panorama of water and the shore beyond was uninterrupted by planting. The orientation is to the southeast, ideal in this climate. Here was an out-of-door living area warmed by the morning sun but shaded from the heat of the day. Here during seven or eight months of the year in Virginia's climate was a truly grand setting for the social activities of the household. Here, we are told, the general took his exercise in inclement weather. The piazza was an innovation that entitles its creator to a place of distinction among planners and design-

THE EAST FRONT OF THE MANSION

Fig. 21. From an engraving by Samuel Seymour after a sketch by William Birch; published in Philadelphia in 1804.
(Courtesy of the Mount Vernon Ladies' Association.)

ers—among architects, if we may have recourse to modern terminology.

BRYAN FAIRFAX—UNCOMMON NEIGHBOR

Bryan Fairfax was as uncommon among his contemporaries as was the newly enlarged Mount Vernon among houses of the period. His career during the war years affords an interesting local sidelight on the measures adopted in Virginia to insure unity on the home front. Youngest son of William

Fairfax of Belvoir, he was a half brother of Anne Fairfax—wife of George Washington's elder half brother Lawrence. His sister, Hannah Fairfax, was the wife of George Washington's cousin, Warner Washington. From early youth he shared the intimate relationship that existed between the Fairfaxes and the Washingtons. His early life was varied and colored by impetuosity. For several years he served a mercantile apprenticeship in the West Indies, but he returned to Virginia in time to be commissioned as a cadet during the French and Indian War. He served with Virginia troops on the frontier under the command of George Washington. Here he first showed signs of a religious mysticism that was to influence his later life. In 1759 he married Elizabeth Cary, younger sister of Sally Cary Fairfax, wife of his elder half brother, George William Fairfax, and established himself at "Towlson Grange," a 5000-acre estate near Great Falls in Fairfax County, which he had inherited from his father. To this inheritance his elder kinsman, Lord Fairfax, proprietor of the Northern Neck, added more than 12,000 adjacent acres. George Washington's diaries for the years before the Revolution record a constant intermingling of the social lives of the two families, despite the distance between Mount Vernon and Towlson.

Particular interest in Bryan Fairfax relates here to the precarious middle ground on which he took position in the struggle between the colonies and the mother country. In 1770 he refused to sign the nonimportation agreement, although he shared the common local resentment of ministerial policy. In 1774 he dissented from the Fairfax Resolves and elaborated his views in a lengthy letter to Washington, which he intended to be read before the county committee. In friendly vein he attempted to persuade Washington to his point of view, and the latter, in the same spirit, affirmed his opposite stand.

The wonder is that the community at large did not make Fairfax's position intolerable. In 1774 and 1775 the county committees throughout Virginia were marshaling every resource at their command to enforce compliance with their decrees and resolves. Upon the outbreak of hostilities and the severance of ties with the mother country, these measures were intensified and given the force of legal enactment. Denouncement was succeeded by test oaths, multiple taxation, imprisonment, exile, and confiscation of property; position and wealth afforded no immunity. The program was so uniformly and aggressively administered in Virginia that latent opposition was stifled before it could find a common voice. The Fairfax County Committee was one of the earliest and most effective in this movement. Bryan Fairfax's exceptional immunity from oppressive measures bespeaks a high degree of esteem on the part of his fellow citizens, unusual respect for his honest convictions, and, perhaps, general emulation of the tolerant attitude of George Washington toward his friend's dissent.

Not content with political dissent, Bryan Fairfax embraced another losing cause late in 1775. On 17 December of that year Lund Washington wrote to his employer:

Mr. Bryan Fairfax has become a preacher. He gave public notice that on such a day he should preach at his own house. Accordingly, on that day many assembled to hear him, but to their great confusion and surprise he advised them to return to the bosom of that church in which they had been brought up, for he had been at much pains in examining the scriptures and the different modes of worshipping the Supreme Being, which was now adopted by many to the disgrace of christianity, and that he found none so pure and undefiled as that prescribed by the canons of the Church of England.

The Church of England was disestablished in Virginia during the war; few ministers remained at their posts. Churches fell into disuse; contents were scattered. Bryan Fairfax was undeterred by these adverse circumstances. In the autumn of 1777 he set out with his son for New York to take ship for England, where he hoped to be ordained. In Lancaster, Pennsylvania, they had the misfortune to be imprisoned as loyalists and were released only on receipt of a pass from General Washington. When Bryan at last reached New York, he refused to take the oath prescribed by British military authorities and was compelled to abandon his mission. Safely home again he wrote to his benefactor, 8 December 1777, "That, at a Time your Popularity was at the highest and mine at the lowest, and when it is so common for Men's Resentments to run high agst those that differ from them in Opinion You should act with your wonted Kindness towards me, hath affected me more than any Favour I have received; and could not be believed by some in N: York, it being above the Run of common Minds."

During the remainder of the war Bryan Fairfax remained in undisturbed security at home. After General Washington's return in 1783, he became a regular and welcome visitor at Mount Vernon once again. In 1789 he was ordained as a minister in the newly established Episcopal Church; for several years thereafter he was rector of Christ Church in Alexandria. In 1793 Bryan succeeded to the family title, becoming eighth Lord Fairfax, but he continued to live quietly at the home of his later years, Mount Eagle, on the south shore of Hunting Creek, overlooking Alexandria. There, in December 1799, George Washington paid his last social call. Ten days later Bryan, Lord Fairfax, was one of the "principal mourners" at Washington's funeral. No other among George Washington's intimates could claim a friendship of greater duration or one more marked by lifelong constancy under trying circumstances.

"WE EXPECT A BLOODY SUMMER"

The general's letters to his intimates in 1776, from Cambridge and later through all the bitter vicissitudes of that year, reflect a rather dismal image of the "Spirit of '76," as it stands forth in the actions and attitudes of many founding fathers. Howe's evacuation of Boston in March was viewed by the patriots as a victory. Congress decreed that a medal be struck and presented to General Washington in commemoration of the event (he did not receive it until nine years later). In a letter to John Augustine, 31 March, the general reported at some length on the military tactics that, aided by the timely "interposition of Providence," had persuaded Howe to abandon Boston. The medal and other pleasing testimonies of approbation of his conduct would in retirement afford "many comfortable reflections," he wrote. Forgotten for the moment were his frustrations as commander of a motley Yankee militia, which had impelled him on 29 August 1775 to write to his fellow Virginian and recent congressional colleague, Richard Henry Lee, that no pecuniary recompense could have induced him to undergo the annoyance and fatigue of his task.

Howe had indeed sailed away after destroying a great store of provisions and munitions, but his force was intact, and a long, inviting coastal area was at the mercy of Britain's combined sea and land forces. As he turned southward toward New York, where he expected the next blow to fall, Washington was hopeful that Congress would honor his urgent pleas for a standing army, enlisted for the duration of the war. He was convinced that only such a force, disciplined, trained and equipped, could stand up to British forces and bring the war to a successful conclusion.

In a letter from Philadelphia at the end of May 1776, he congratulated his brother John Augustine on the Virginia Convention's resolution instructing their delegates in the Congress to move for independence. He held no hope of accommodation with the mother country and deplored the fact that so many, including members of Congress, "are still feeding themselves on the dainty food of reconciliation. . . . We expect a bloody summer of it in New York and Canada. . . . We are not, either in men or arms, prepared for it," he wrote. He believed, however, that Providence would continue to afford her aid.

On 9 July, at his headquarters in New York, in general orders for the day, the commander-in-chief announced that the Congress had declared "the United Colonies of North America free and Independent States." The army was urged to act with fidelity and courage, with an awareness that peace and safety depended, "under God," solely on the success of their arms. The Declaration of Independence was indeed a brave document. The colonies declared their independence, but they were not effectively united; the Articles of Confederation and Perpetual Union, adopted and dispatched to the states for ratification in November 1777, did not become operative until the last state, Maryland, ratified the compact on 1 March 1781. Even then the Congress did not have powers equal to its responsibilities.

General Washington's next letter to Brother John, 22 July 1776, painted an ominous picture. His force in New York, numbering about 15,000, confronted a powerful British fleet. A force of 8000 or 9000 British troops on Staten Island was expected soon to total 25,000, as reinforcements disembarked. Two British warships had already successfully run the gauntlet of his shore batteries and moved up the Hudson River to menace his lines of communication and supply.

On 19 August the general reported to Lund that his strength had been increased to 23,000 by the arrival of militia. General Howe was believed to have between 20,000 and 27,000 men, soon to be augmented by 5000 Hessians. He could not understand why Howe continued to temporize. The season for campaigning was far advanced, and he held only one small island, "which it was never the intention of the Americans to dispute . . . a small step towards the Conquest of this Continent." The two British warships above the city, having been menaced by fire ships, had retreated downriver.

On 22 September, from the Heights of Harlem, he wrote at length to John Augustine about the "attack and Retreat from Long Island." He wrote with restraint of the two detachments that "in a great measure" occasioned the Long Island defeat by allowing themselves to be surprised and retreating precipitately. Of the withdrawal from Long Island, a masterly operation conducted under his own direction, he noted only that it "was effected without loss of Men, and with but very little baggage." The evacuation of Manhattan Island he explained as a necessary measure. His account of the disgraceful panic at Kip's Bay, in the course of this retreat, reported his personal involvement in tempered language, "I used every possible effort to rally them, but to no purpose . . . they ran off without firing a Single Gun." In later skirmishes some of the troops behaved well, but the dependence that Congress placed on the militia had already been greatly injurious, and, he feared, would bring total ruin. "In short, it is not in the power of Words to describe the task I have to act. £50,000 should not induce me again to undergo what I have done."

On 30 September, from Colonel Morris's on the Heights of Harlem, Washington wrote to Lund:

The amazement which you seem to be in at the unaccountable measures which have been adopted by—[Congress] would be a good deal increased if I had time to unfold the whole system of their management since this time twelve months. I do not know how to account for the unfortunate steps which have been taken but from that fatal idea of conciliation which prevailed so long— fatal I call it, because from my soul I wish it may [not] prove so, though my fears lead me to think there is too much danger of it.

He cited recent experience which proved the extravagance and the fallacy of depending on militia and short-term enlistments in the Continental army. He continued:

In short, such is my situation that if I were to wish the bitterest curse to an enemy on this side of the grave, I should put him in my place with my feelings; yet I do not know what plan of conduct to pursue. I see the impossibility of serving with reputation, or doing any essential service to the cause by continuing in command, and yet I am told that if I quit the command inevitable ruin will follow from the distraction that will ensue. . . . But I will be done with the subject, with the precaution to you that it is not a fit one to be known or discussed. If I fall, it may not be amiss that these circumstances be known, and declaration made in justice to the credit of my character.

In a letter to Governor Patrick Henry a few days later (5 October), the general urged that the officers selected for the Continental battalion about to be raised in Virginia should have "a just pretention to the Character of a Gentleman, a proper sense of Honor, and some reputation to lose." These were the qualifications that he had found wanting in the militia officers from states north of Mason and Dixon's line. It was his belief that the militia would fight very well if properly officered—that if they had been properly conducted and supported at Bunker Hill, the British would have suffered a decisive defeat with greater casualties.

Despite his lack of faith in his troops, Washington was willing to stand his ground on Harlem Heights, knowing that militia were more dependable when entrenched, as at Bunker Hill, with an inviting opportunity to make the most of their marksmanship. He would chance the issue in the hope that his presence might make a decisive difference. But General Howe also had a keen recollection of Bunker Hill and wisely avoided the possibility of another disastrous victory in a similar setting by moving a strong force through Hells Gate into the East River and landing at a point from which he could threaten the American army on Harlem Heights with encirclement.

In a letter to John Augustine that was begun at White Plains on 6 November and completed at Hackensack, New Jersey, on the nineteenth, General Washington brought the account of his military adventures up to date. Howe's sudden landing with about 16,000 men at Throg's or Frog's Neck on the East River had obliged the American army on the Heights of Harlem "to remove our Camp and out Flank him, which we have done, and by degrees got strongly posted on advantageous Ground at this place."

Resuming his narrative at Hackensack thirteen days later Washington reported that Howe, finding the Americans strongly positioned and ready to receive his attack at White Plains, had filed off and retreated toward New York. Fearing that Howe would move into New Jersey, then on to Philadelphia, Washington had divided his dwindling force, leaving Gen. Charles Lee to maneuver east of the Hudson above New York. Three thousand men were stationed at Peekskill and the Highland passes to defend the river. Washington, with about 5000 men, hastened to cross into New Jersey by a roundabout upriver march, the lower ferries being denied to him by British men-of-war.

Washington notes that he did not get across the river in time to save Fort Washington on upper Manhatten Island, which had fallen on 16 November. He quotes from General Greene's report, "Colo. Magaw could not get the Men to Man the lines, otherwise he would not have given up the Fort."

Washington confessed that it was "a most unfortunate affair, and has given me great Mortification as we have lost not only two thousand men that were there, but a good deal of artillery, and some of the best arms we had." The fort was held, he notes, contrary to his wishes and opinion, the decision having been made by a full Council of General Officers, influenced by the strong desire of the Congress that obstruction of the river should be prolonged.

"I am wearied almost to death with the retrograde Motions of things," he wrote, "and I solumnly protest that a pecuniary reward of £20,000 a year would not induce me to undergo what I do."

Had he held his letter to John Augustine twenty-four hours longer, he could have added another melancholy note by reporting that the British had captured Fort Lee, on the Jersey shore of the river opposite Fort Washington. The garrison got away, but there was a heavy loss of munitions, baggage, tents, about a thousand barrels of flour, and other stores.

"DESPARATE DISEASES REQUIRE DESPARATE REMEDIES"

On 10 December 1776, at "Falls of Delaware So. Side," General Washington commenced two letters to Lund, both to be laid aside under pressure of more urgent matters, and not to be completed until the 17th, "ten miles above the Falls." One of these letters, acknowledging Lund's letters of 20 and 26 October, is a disjointed document, reflecting the distracting circumstances under which it was written. Its content reflects, also, a possible cause-and-effect relationship between the fortunes of war and contingencies at Mount Vernon. He advised in detail about providing horses for Mrs. Washington's chariot, evincing his concern that she should have dependable transportation:

Matters to my view, but this I say in confidence to you, as a friend, wear so unfavorable aspect (not that I apprehend so much danger from Howes Army as from the disaffection of the three states of New York, Jersey and Pennsylvania) that I would look forward to unfavorable Events, and prepare Accordingly in such a manner however as to give no alarm or suspicion to anyone; as one step toward it, have my Papers in such a Situation as to remove at a short notice in case an Enemy's Fleet should come up the River. When they are removed let them go immediately to my Brother's in Berkeley.

The remainder of this letter touches briefly on clothing for the Negroes and offers detailed advice on ornamental plantings about the mansion. These topics must have afforded him an enjoyable respite, however brief, from the urgent problems which beset him.

The general's second letter of the same dates to Lund gives a brief account of his retreat across New Jersey with a dwindling force and his situation on the west bank of the Delaware. We might look elsewhere for a more objective evaluation of these events and the part played by George Washington, but this fact in no way diminishes the interest or the historical importance of his own narrative:

> Falls of Delaware, South Side
> December 10, 1776

Dear Lund:

I wish to Heaven it was in my power to give you a more favorable account of our situation than it is. Our numbers, quite inadequate to the task of opposing that part of the army under the command of General Howe, being reduced by sickness, desertion, and political deaths (on or before the first instant, and having no assistance from the militia), [we] were obliged to retire before the enemy, who were perfectly well informed of our situation, till we came to this place, where I have no idea of being able to make a stand, as my numbers, till joined by the Philadelphia militia, did not exceed three thousand men fit for duty. Now we may be about five thousand to oppose Howe's whole army, that part of it excepted which sailed under the command of Gen. Clinton. I tremble for Philadelphia. Nothing, in my opinion, but Gen. Lee's speedy arrival, who has been long expected, though still at a distance (with about three thousand men), can save it. We have brought over and destroyed all the boats we could lay our hands on upon the Jersey shore for many miles above and below this place; but it is next to impossible to guard a shore for sixty miles, with less than half the enemy's numbers; when by force or strategem they may suddenly attempt a passage in many different places. At present they are encamped or quartered along the other shore and below us (rather this place, for we are obliged to keep a face towards them) for fifteen miles.

December 17, ten miles above
the Falls.

I have since moved up to this place, to be more convenient to our great and extensive defences of this river. Hitherto, by our destruction of the boats, and vigilance in watching the fords of the river above the falls (which are now rather high), we have prevented them from crossing; but how long we shall be able to do it God only knows, as they are still hovering about the river. And if every thing else fails, will wait till the 1st of January, when there will be no other men to oppose them but militia, none of which but those from Philadelphia, mentioned in the first part of the letter, are yet come (although I am told some are expected from the back counties). When I say none but militia, I am to except the Virginia regiments and the shattered remains of Smallwood's, which, by fatigue, want of clothes, &c., are reduced to nothing—Weedon's, which was the strongest, not having more than between one hundred and thirty to one hundred and forty men fit for duty, the rest being in the hospitals. The unhappy policy of short enlistments and a dependence upon militia will, I fear, prove the downfall of our cause, though early pointed out with an almost prophetic spirit! Our cause has also received a severe blow in the captivity of Gen. Lee. Unhappy man! Taken by his own imprudence, going three or four miles from his own camp, and within twenty of the enemy, notice of which by a rascally Tory was given a party of light horse seized him in the morning after travelling all night, and carried him off in high triumph and with every mark of indignity, not even suffering him to get his hat or surtout coat. The troops that were under his command are not yet come up with us, though they, I think, may be expected to-morrow. A large part of the Jerseys have given every proof of disaffection that they can do, and this part of Pennsylvania are equally inimical. In short, your imagination can scarce extend to a situation more distressing than mine. Our only dependence now is upon the speedy enlistment of a new army. If this fails, I think the game will be pretty well up, as, from disaffection and want of spirit and fortitude, the inhabitants, instead of resistance, are offering submission and taking protection from Gen. Howe in Jersey. I am &c.

Washington's letter of 18 December to Brother John differs little in tone or content from his earlier letter to Lund. The conduct of the Jerseys had been "Infamous," and if every nerve is not strained to recruit a new army, he thinks "the game is pretty near up," as he stated to Lund. "However under a full persuasion of the justice of our Cause I cannot entertain an Idea that it will finally sink, tho' it may remain for some time under a Cloud."

Here begins a gap of over fourteen months in the surviving letters of George Washington to his Mount Vernon manager. Nor is there an extant letter to brother John Augustine earlier than 24 February 1777, by which time the Trenton-Princeton campaign was no longer news. His letter of 22 January 1777 from Morristown to his stepson, John Parke Custis, states that they might have cleared the Jerseys entirely of the enemy if more Continental troops had been prevailed upon to stay beyond the expiration of their enlistments and the militia had responded in time. "In my letter to Lund Washington," he wrote, "I have given the late occurrences, and to avoid repetition, I refer you to him." By the disappearance of this letter to Lund we are denied George Washington's firsthand, private account of the battles of Trenton and Princeton, which reversed the tide of events.

On 20 December 1776, in a long letter to Congress, which had removed to Baltimore, Washington had warned that ten more days would put an end to the army. "Desparate diseases require Desparate Remedies," he wrote, in asking for enlarged powers. Looking back over the wearying chain of events since Boston had been regained, it was evident to him that the defense of Long Island had been worse than futile, Kip's Bay had been a disgrace, White Plains had been a standoff—but a humiliating one, in that he would not have dared to stand his ground—Fort Washington was a major disaster, and the retreat through New Jersey bore the aspects of a final collapse. On 23 December the New York *Mercury*, a tory sheet, reported that "Mr. Washington, with about two thousand poor wretches . . . has fled to Lancaster in Pennsylvania." This was untrue but would have seemed all too plausible to friend or foe. The next stage seemed inevitable. The Continental army would cease to exist on 31 December, and the British, who had gone into winter quarters at Trenton, Princeton, and Brunswick with orders to be in readiness to assemble on short notice, would cross the Delaware on the ice or by boat, brush aside a dispirited force of militia, and occupy Philadelphia. But George Washington was not reconciled to the inevitable; he invoked a "desparate remedy." On Christmas night he recrossed the Delaware with about twenty-four hundred Continentals, surprised the Hessians at Trenton, and recrossed the river with nearly a thousand prisoners. A dying cause was given new life.

No letter from Lund to George Washington survives for this period to record the reaction at Mount Vernon to this victory, but the diary of Nicholas Cresswell, English loyalist, records the reaction in Northern Virginia to the news of the patriot triumph:

Scotland, Loudoun County Virginia—Monday, Jan. 6th, 1777. News that Washington has taken 760 Hessian prisoners at Trenton in the Jerseys. Hope it is a lie. This afternoon hear he has likewise taken six pieces of Brass Cannon. *Tuesday, Jan. 7th,* 1777. The news is confirmed. The minds of the people are much altered. A few days ago they had given up the cause for lost. Their late successes have turned the scale and now they are all liberty mad again. Their Recruiting parties could not get a man (except he bought him from his master) no longer since than last week, and now the men are coming in by companies. Confound the turncoat scoundrels and the cowardly Hessians together. This has given them new spirits, got them fresh succours and will prolong the War, perhaps for two years. They have recovered their panic and it will not be an easy matter to throw them into that confusion again. Volunteer Companies are collecting in every County on the Continent and in a few months the rascals will be stronger than ever.

General Cornwallis had been on the point of sailing for home to report to the ministry that the rebels were crushed and the rebellion was at an end. His baggage was retrieved from the ship, and he hurried back to the British headquarters at Brunswick to resume command.

On 27 December the Continental Congress granted General Washington the enlarged powers he had requested, and more. He was authorized to raise, officer, and equip a new army; to take, wherever he might be, whatever he might want for the use of the army; to arrest and confine those who refused to take the continental currency and other disaffected persons. These powers were to vest in the general for six months. At the same time he was authorized to offer bounties to soldiers who would stay in service beyond the terms of their enlistment.

On 30 December Washington, not yet aware of his new powers, had crossed the Delaware once again, determined to apply another "desparate Remedy" if the Continentals would stay with him for another six weeks. These men, about twenty-four hundred, were paraded; a ten-dollar bounty was offered. About half of the men accepted. This tiny remnant of the Continental army was reinforced by about thirty-four hundred militia, most of whom had never heard a rifle fired in anger. On the night of 2 January 1777, this mixed force was positioned on the south bank of a shallow creek, across from Trenton, confronting Cornwallis's formidable force, which had driven their stubbornly resisting skirmishers out of the town. The British general looked forward eagerly to a decisive battle the next day. But at midnight the Americans abandoned their lines, leaving a small force to keep their campfires burning brightly, marched round Cornwallis's left flank, and moved on Princeton. There, in a bloody clash, they defeated and scattered the three regiments that had been posted to defend the town. With 300 prisoners Washington moved on to a secure encampment at Morristown, where he went into winter quarters. The British forces were withdrawn to Brunswick and Perth Amboy. On 20 January, in a report to the home government, Lord Howe wrote, "I do not now see a prospect of terminating the war but by a general action, and am aware of the difficulty in our way to obtain it, as the enemy moves with so much more celerity than we possibly can."

In his official correspondence Washington referred modestly to the capture of the Hessian garrison at Trenton as "our late lucky blow"; the battle of Princeton was "this piece of good fortune." To Congress he expressed the opinion that six or eight hundred fresh troops could have taken Brunswick with its stores and military chest and "put an end to the war." This is debatable, but the cause had been saved in a remarkable turnabout.

STALEMATE

In a letter of 24 February 1777 to brother John Augustine from Morristown, General Washington reported that "nothing of any great Importance has occur'd of late." If Howe is a general of any enterprise, there would be events of consequence, as circumstances were very favorable to the British, but on this topic, he noted, it would be indiscreet to enlarge in a letter that might miscarry. The militia was as undependable as ever, "here today, and gone tomorrow." Desertion was a growing evil. There were frequent skirmishes between his own forces and enemy foraging parties, in which the enemy always sustained a greater loss in killed and wounded, owing to the Americans' superior skill in firearms, "but this is counterbalanced by a set of Parracides who have engaged in their Service, and Inlist all our Country men they can Seduce." His circumspect account of the situation ended on a qualified expression of optimism, "If we can once get the New Army compleat and the Congress will take care to have it properly supplied, I think we may, thereafter, bid Defiance to Great Britain, and her foreign Auxiliaries."

In a letter of the same date to Governor Patrick Henry, General Washington earnestly entreated that the troops raised in Virginia for the Continental army should be forwarded without delay, as well equipped as possible. In this letter he tactfully alluded to the Virginia legislature's dispatch of John Walker to headquarters to keep it informed of events. There were secrets, he noted, that should not be entrusted to paper, some in fact that should be known only to the commander-in-chief. He had solved the problem and avoided the precedent by taking Walker into his military family as an extra aide-de-camp.

Martha Washington arrived at Morristown in mid-March. She found the general recovering from an illness that had laid him low earlier in the month. Despite his indisposition, an aide noted, he had been "much pestered with things that could not be avoided." Another wrote that he had been irritable. With Martha once again presiding at his dinner table, life assumed a more cheerful aspect. Mrs. Washington brought together officers' wives who had come to visit their husbands at headquarters. One of these, Mrs. Theodorick Bland, the wife of a Virginia colonel, has left in a letter to a friend a rare gossipy account of the social scene at Morristown, with brief descriptions of the military aides. Col. John Fitzgerald of Alexandria was "an agreeable, broad-shouldered Irishman." Col. George Johnston, another Virginian, was exceedingly witty at other people's expense, but couldn't allow others to be so at his own. Col. Alexander Hamilton was "a sensible, genteel young fellow." Col. Richard Meade, another Virginian, is named without comment; he was probably known to her correspondent. Col. Tench Tilghman of Maryland was "a modest, worthy man, who from his attachment to the General lives in his family and acts in any capacity that is uppermost, without fee or reward." Col. Robert Harrison was a brother of Billy Harrison, who kept a store in Petersburg, Virginia, and, much like him, a worthy man. Capt. Caleb Gibbs of the headquarters guard was "a good natured Yankee who makes a thousand blunders in the Yankee style and keeps the dinner table in constant laugh." They were all "polite sociable gentlemen who make the day pass with a great deal of satisfaction to the visitors." There were riding parties after dinner, and the "agreeable Commander" joined the cavalcade when not detained by urgent military matters, at which times he "throws off the hero and takes on the chatty, agreeable companion—he can be down right impudent sometimes—such impudence, Fanny, as you and I like." In these pleasant intervals the citizen-soldier found some compensation for the social life at Mount Vernon that he so sorely missed.

On 3 May 1777, General Washington dispatched an urgent request from Morristown to Dr. William Shippen, Jr.—director general of military hospitals, with headquarters in Philadelphia—for sufficient "Jallap" [jalap] and calomel to treat all his Mount Vernon dependents. Lund's latest letter had reported an outbreak of smallpox among them. All were to be inoculated; the jalap and calomel were to be administered as laxatives in accordance with the prevailing medical practice of the period. From other sources we learn that smallpox was epidemic in northern Virginia at the time. Under date of 20 April Nicholas Cresswell noted in his diary that all the Alexandrians and a regiment of soldiers stationed in the town were undergoing inoculation. "Such a pock-eyed place I never was in before," he wrote.

In a letter of June 1st to John Augustine the general expressed the hope that he and his family had come safely through inoculation:

" . . . the loss my Brother Sam has sustained will I fear, be very sensibly felt by him. Some mismanagement must surely have been in the way, for the Small Pox by Inoculation appears to me to be nothing; my whole Family, I understand, are likely to get well through the disorder with no other assistance than that of Doctor

Lund. In short, one of the best Physicians in this Army has assurd me, that the great skill which many of the faculty pretend to have in the management of this disorder, and the great Art necessary to treat the patient well, is neither more nor less than a cheat upon the World; that in general an old Woman may Inoculate with as much success as the best Physician."

Brother Sam had lost his fourth wife, a victim of the mortality that sometimes resulted from inept inoculation or unforeseen complications. The regiment undergoing inoculation in Alexandria may have been a unit on its way to join the Continental army. Urgent as was his need for reinforcements, the Commander had established inoculation centers at intermediate points before incorporating recruits into his army.

On 10 May Tilghman noted in a letter from Morristown to his father that Mrs. Washington would set out for Philadelphia in a day or two and that he expected to attend her to that city. This was the shortest of her annual wartime sojourns with the general at the winter quarters of the Continental Army. Her invitation to Morristown had been withheld until it became apparent that Howe was too comfortably settled in New York to mount a winter offensive against the rebel encampment. Her departure was prompted by the general's need to put his forces in a state of readiness for offensive or defensive maneuvers as his lethargic adversary commenced to rouse from his prolonged state of hibernation.

On 10 June the general wrote to Mrs. Washington under cover to Maj. Gen. Thomas Mifflin with a request that his letter be delivered to her if she was still in Philadelphia; if not, it was to be forwarded to Virginia. While in Philadelphia the general's lady may have taken possession of the handsome coach that the state of Pennsylvania purchased for her use from Richard Penn, Esq., governor of Pennsylvania, 1771–73. That gentlemen had left the coach behind when he returned to England in 1775. The bill of sale, embodying a detailed description of the vehicle, is dated 14 June 1777. This coach, however well-intended the gift, would have been over-heavy for the severe punishment it would have been subjected to by the roads of the period and too ornate for any but state occasions. How much service it saw in the war years and later cannot be determined from the surviving records. Another hiatus in the account of Mrs. Washington's wartime travels and her social and cultural diversions along the way denies us the answer to another question of minor moment, but one that invites speculation. Did she hear one of the public concerts being given that summer in Philadelphia by the Hessian military band that had been captured at Trenton in the early morning of 26 December 1776? Her pleasure in the occasion, if it occurred, would have been many-faceted. We may assume that she would have enjoyed the music. As a loyal subscriber to the principles set forth in the Declaration of Independence, she would also have been pleased that the bandmen had been liberated from the bondage to the king of England into which they had been sold by their own tyrannical prince. And, best of all, she could have taken pride in the band as a trophy that her warrior husband had brought back from the field of battle. The date of her departure for Viginia is not recorded.

For George Washington the summer of 1777 was a period of continued frustration. General Howe and his brother, the admiral, with a superior land force and undisputed command of the sea, had all of the options. It was obvious that the British and Hessians could march from northern New Jersey to Philadelphia as easily as they had marched to the Delaware in 1776. More logically, it seemed, they would move up the Hudson to effect a junction with Burgoyne, who was moving southward from Canada, with Albany as his objective. With British control of the Hudson, New England would be cut off from the central and southern states. But it could not be reliably assumed on the basis of past performance that the enemy would act logically. Washington was beset by problems that had become perennial, as he had confided in a letter to brother John Augustine from Morristown on April 12, "The Campaign will, I expect, be opened without men on our side, unless they come in much faster than I expect them." Even the basic plan that he had determined to pursue—a war of attrition, of skirmishes and raids, avoiding at all times a general engagement unless the odds were heavily in his favor—could not be waged without men.

When Howe withdrew from northern New Jersey and began embarking his forces, Washington could not convince himself that his destination was not up the Hudson. "By means of their Shipping and easy transportation that shipping affords, they have it much in their power to lead us a very disagreeable dance," he wrote to John Augustine on 29 June from Middlebrook. On 5 August from Germantown he reported to his brother that his troops were much harassed and fatigued by marching and countermarching. When Howe's fleet appeared at the Capes of Delaware, they had marched from positions near West Point on the Hudson to the defense of Philadelphia. Now the fleet had disappeared. In a postscript dated 9 August he noted that the fleet was still unreported, and he was about to move slowly northward. This movement was halted when news came that the British fleet had been sighted off Maryland's Eastern Shore. Another anxious period of suspense ensued until Howe's purpose was fully disclosed by his presence far up Chesapeake Bay.

On 11 September the British and American forces, nearly equal in numbers, met in battle at Brandywine Creek. Washington's right wing under General Sullivan was outflanked as it had been at Long Island in 1776 under the command of this same general. Once again trained professionals triumphed over militia and partially trained Continentals. While Brandywine was a defeat, there was no rout, and the American forces were not disspirited. Three weeks later these same troops launched a vigorous surprise attack on Howe's forces at Germantown. The surprise was complete, but once again lack of discipline was a handicap. An early-morning autumnal fog made things difficult for both sides, but it was American units that ran out of ammunition; two American brigades mistakenly fired on one another in the fog. The British rallied, and the Americans retreated. For the moment Providence seemed to have changed sides, but the morale of Washington's troops was raised. They had driven the British regulars, and they believed that, but for the fog, they would have won a complete victory.

Under date of 18 October to brother John Augustine, the general reported details of the British victories at Brandywine and Germantown. In a postscript he quoted a dispatch just received from Albany bringing "important and glorious News":

Albany, October 15, 1777.

Last night at 8 o'Clock the Capitulation, whereby Genl. Burgoyne and the whole Army surrendered themselves Prisoners of War, was signed, and this morning they are to march out towards the River above fish Creek with the honours of war (and there ground their Arms) they are from thence to be marched to Massachusetts Bay. We congratulate you on this happy event, and remain. Yours &ca.
Geo. Clinton.

Later in October, in a letter to Landon Carter of Sabine Hall in Westmoreland County, Virginia, Washington contrasted the circumstances that contributed to General Gates's victory at Saratoga with the apathy and feeble local support that contributed to his defeats at Brandywine and Germantown: "Genl. Gates was reenforced by upwards of 12000 Militia who shut the only door by which Burgoyne could Retreat, and cut off all his supplies. How different our case! the disaffection of great part of the Inhabitants of this State, the languor of others and internal distraction of the whole, have been among the great and insuperable difficulties I have met with." He does not complain, but flatters himself that "a Superintending Providence is ordering everything for the best and that, in due time all will end well." After Germantown, the two opposed armies marched, halted, and skirmished inconclusively. The British fleet gained control of the Delaware from the capes to Philadelphia, and Howe settled comfortably into that city. General Washington, with the remnants of his army, hungry and threadbare, went into winter quarters at Valley Forge.

After a respite of unrecorded duration at Mount Vernon, Mrs. Washington had gone on to New Kent County for a visit with her sister, Anna Maria (Nancy), and her brother-in-law, Burwell Bassett, at "Eltham." The *Virginia Gazette* of 2 August 1777 reports that she visited Williamsburg also. "Lady Washington, the amiable consort of his excellency General Washington, came to town from Eltham, the seat of Burwell Bassett, Esq. in New Kent," the account states. "Upon her arrival she was saluted with the firing of cannon and small arms, and was safely conducted to Mrs. Dawson's in the city." It must have reminded the amiable lady of her reception in Philadelphia en route to Cambridge. These old friends and neighbors were also treating her as though she were "A Great Somebody"!

In a letter from Willimsburg to General Washington on 22 August, Mrs. Washington's brother, Bartholomew Dandridge, notes that he is sending the general's letter to Martha on to Eltham. He reports that all are well there except "Mr. Custis's little girl" (Mrs. Washington's infant granddaughter, Eliza). On her return to Mount Vernon, Mrs. Washington took the Bassetts' two young sons, Burwell, Jr., age thirteen, and John, twelve, with her to be inoculated for smallpox.

Under date of 18 November, Martha wrote to her sister that the boys "have had the small pox exceeding light and have been perfectly well for this fortnight past." They have also "been exceeding good boys indeed." She had paid the doctor's fee, £9. "The Doctor's charge is very high but I did not say a word—he carried the children so well through the small pox." This long, affectionate family letter makes only one brief reference to the war: "The last letter I had from the General was dated the 7th of this month—he says nothing has happened since the unsuccessful attack upon our forts on the Delawar."

Anna Maria Bassett died at Eltham a short time after the return of her young sons from Mount Vernon, carrying the letter quoted. Mrs. Washington's letter of condolence to her bereaved husband says, "She was the greatest favorite I had in the world." She wanted to be helpful in any way possible.

"My dear sister in her life time often mentioned my taking my dear Fanny (ten years old) if she should be taken away before she grew up—if you will let her come to live with me, I will with the greatest pleasure take her and be a parent and mother to her as long as I live—and will come down for her as soon as I come from northward,—The General has wrote to me that he can not come home this winter but as soon as the army under his command goes into winter quarters he will send for me, if he does I must goe,—if he does not, I will come down as soon as Nelly Custis gets well. She is here and expects every day to be brought to bed—is the reason I can not come down at this time." Nelly Custis's second child, Martha, was born at Mount Vernon on 31 December.

Fanny Bassett did not join the Mount Vernon family until Christmas Eve, 1784. She was by this time a charming young lady of seventeen. Fanny was to become a second daughter to her Aunt Martha, filling a void caused by the death of her own daughter, Patsy, in 1773.

VALLEY FORGE AND THE CONWAY CABAL

In late January of 1778 Mrs. Washington set out from Mount Vernon over frozen roads, with a neighbor, Capt. Thomas Triplett, to join her husband at Valley Forge. She arrived on 2 or 3 February, having been met enroute by Colonel Meade, who was sent to escort her to headquarters. On 7 March she wrote to her friend Mercy Warren, wife of James Warren of Massachusetts. "The general is encamped in what is called the great valley on the Banks of the Schuykill. Officers and men are chiefly in Hutts, which they say is tolerable comfortable; the army are as healthy as can well be expected in general. The General's apartment is very small; he has had a log cabben built to dine in which has made our quarter much more tolerable than they were at first."

Before her departure from Mount Vernon Mrs. Washington had received from Dr. James Craik a letter that he had written to the general. She was requested to forward it under cover of one of her own. It was an important letter, and the doctor had reason to believe that it was less likely to be diverted or delayed if Mrs. Washington were to enclose it with one of her regular missives.

James Craik was born in Scotland. He studied medicine at Edinburgh and emigrated at the age of twenty, practicing for a brief period in the West Indies before coming to Virginia. He had served with Washington in the French and Indian War; at Monongahela he attended the mortally wounded Braddock. Dr. Craik and Col. George Washington were rewarded by the Virginia Assembly for gallant and meritorious conduct at this battle. (See fig. 22.) After the war Craik had married and settled on a plantation at Port Tobacco, Maryland, a few miles downriver from Mount Vernon. In 1770 he had accompanied Washington on a journey into the wilds along the Ohio and Kanawha Rivers to locate lands for allotment, under a grant from the Crown to the officers and men who had served in the French and Indian War. In 1777 Dr. Craik was appointed assistant director general of the hospital department of the army. From Port Tobacco, the doctor wrote:

Portobacco Maryland Jany 6th, 1778

Dear Sir

Notwithstanding your unwearied diligence and the unparalleled Sacrifice of Domestic happiness and ease of mind which you have made for the good of our Country yet you are not wanting in Secret Enemeis who would Rob you of the great and truely deserved Esteem your County has for you. Base and Villainous men thro' Chagrin, Envy, or Ambition, are endeavouring to lessen you in the minds of the people and taking underhanded methods to traduce your Character.—The morning I left Camp I was informed by a Gentleman, whom I believe to be a true Friend of yours, that a Strong Faction was forming against you in the New board of War and in the Congress. It alarmed me exceedingly, and I wished that he had informed me of it a day or two sooner; that I might have taken an opportunity of mentioning it to you. He begged that I would do it before I went away; but upon Consideration I thought I had best defer it untill I reached home, perhaps I might make some further discoveries on my way. At my Arrival in Bethlehem I was told of it there, and was told that I should hear more of it on my way down. I did so, for at Lancaster I was still assured of it. All the way down I heard it, and I believe it is pretty general over the Country. no one would pretend to affix it on particulars, yet all seemed to believe it. it was said some of the Eastern & Southern Members, were at the bottom of it, particularly one who has been said to be your Enemy before, but denied it, R.H.L. and that G——l M——n in the New Board of War was a very active person. This last I am afraid is too true. I think I have reason to believe him not your Friend from many Circumstances.—The method they are taking is by holding up General G——s to the people and making them believe that you have had three or four times the number of the Enemy, and have done nothing, that Philadelphia was given up by your mismanagement and that you have missed many opportunities of defeating the Enemy, and many other things as ungenerous & unjust.—These are the low artifices they are making use of. It is said that they dare not appear openly as your Enemy, but that the New Board of War is Composed of such leading men as will throw such obstacles and difficulties in your way as to force you to resign. Had I not been assured of those things from such Authority as I cannot doubt it, I should not have troubled you with this. My attachment to your Person is Such, my Friendship is so Sincere that every Hint which has a tendency to hurt your Honour wounds me most Sensibly. And I write this that you may be apprized, and have an Eye toward those men, and particularly that man G——l M——n. He is Plausible, Sensible, Popular and Ambitious, takes great pains to draw over every Officer he meets to his own way of thinking and is very engaging. The above I can with sincerity say I have wrote from pure motives of Friendship and have no Enmity to any of those men, any farther than they are Enemies to you. If they are your Enemies every honest man must naturally conclude they are Enemies to the Country and the Glorious Cause in which we are engaged, and will no Doubt most Streneously exert every Nerve to disappoint their Villainous intentions.

On my calling at Mr. Booths in Frederick Maryland I found my Eldest Son recovering from a fever in which he has been dangerously ill for several Weeks; and for several days was expected every hour to die. On my arrival at home I found Mrs. Craik in a very low & poor state of health which she has been in for Some time past. She still continues in a weak & low Condition, which I am afraid will put it out of my power to join the Army as soon as I could wish. If she does not recover her health I shall be under the disagreeable necessity of Resigning my appointment as I cannot think of leaving her in a bad State of health with Such a large family. Should she recover her health Soon I shall loose no time in geting to Camp but her Situation alarms me much at present. I get the favour of Mrs. Washington to send this under Cover to you as I expect it will be the most Safe and Expeditious Conveyance as her letters Seldom Miscarry. May God of his infinite mercy Protect & Defend you from all your open and Secret Enemies and Continue you in health to finish the Glorious undertaking is the Sincere Prayers of

Your Most Devoted & Obliged hum. Svt.

Jas. Craik

Mrs. Craik offers her most respectful Comps. to you

Of the "Base and Villainous men" identified by Dr. Craik, Richard Henry Lee (RHL) was less culpable than the other two he pointed out, Maj. Gen. Thomas Mifflin (G——l M——n) and Maj. Gen. Gates (G——l G——s). Nonetheless, Lee was widely suspected in Virginia of being implicated in the plot, which has been labeled by historians as the Conway Cabal. In his letter of 18 February 1778 to his employer, Lund Washington dwelt on this topic at some length:

Colonel Mason (who I showed your letter of the 16th of January) tells me he was informed of the cabal against you before he left Williamsburg and some had hinted to him that R.H. Lee was one suspected of having a hand in it, and as they knew the intimacy existing between them, begged that he would talk to Lee and discover whether anything of the sort was in agitation or not. He did so. And that Lee declares no such thing or even a hint has ever been mentioned in Congress, and that he should look upon it as one of the greatest misfortunes that could befall this continent, should you by any means whatever give up the command of the Army, for fully convinced he was in his own opinion no other man

GENERAL WASHINGTON'S DESK AND CHAIR

Fig. 22. To my compatriot in arms, and old & intimate friend Doctor Craik, I give my Bureau (or as the Cabinet makers call it, Tambour Secretary) and the circular chair—an appendage of my Study.
Last Will and Testament of George Washington.
(Courtesy of the Mount Vernon Ladies' Association.)

upon this continent was equal to the task; that he had often lamented the heavy burden you bare, and the difficulties you had to surmount more than any man ever had before. For his part he looked upon it as one among the many favors we had received from above, that the Supreme Being had been pleased to save and protect in the most miraculous degree the only man in whom every one could confide in. Mason is of opinion it is a Tory menoeuver for he thinks no friend to America can be an enemy to you, for by God, which was his expression, there is not nòr ever was in the world a man who acted from a more laudable and disinterested motive than you do, and that he defied all history to show a war, begun, and carried on, under more disadvantages than the present; nor, he would venture to affirm one that had been better conducted so far as it depended on the Commander-in-Chief, for that he had observed you had foreseen and pointed out what would be the event of all the blunders committed by the different Legislators, and that whereever you had given your opinion the event had proved you were right, then enumerated a number of instances to prove his assertion. Mason concluded by saying that he was convinced from the whole of his conversation with Lee, Harrison and other members of Congress, that a faction in Congress against you had never existed. Our conversation passed in Alexandria before several gentlemen, among whom was Major Jennifer of Maryland.

A month later, 18 March, Lund returned to the cabal and the question of R. H. Lee's involvement:

Happy I am to hear that shame and disgrace is likely to fall on your secret enemys. Mr. Custis came up from Williamsburg last night. He tells me he was a day or two with the Governor whilst below. That he told him he had pushed R.H.L. very close several times and that he had declared in the most solemn manner his innocence or that there was a design or intention by any of the members of Congress that he knows of to displace you. In short he talked to the Governor as he did to Mason. Colonel Nelson openly and publicly charged and taxed him with it, but he again in the most solemn manner denied it. The Freeholders of King William will not give their votes unless the candidate promises to prevent if possible R.H.L. from ever being in any public office. Some of the countys refused to be draughted unless they were first assured that you were at the head of the Army. If R.H.L.'s innocent it is a pity he should lay under the suspicion of guilt.

The charge against R. H. Lee may be based on nothing more than guilt by association, but his professed ignorance of the existence of a clique in the Continental Congress opposed to the commander-in-chief seems incredible. Some of its members were his close and intimate friends.

As Dr. Craik noted, the Conway Cabal was rooted in the chagrin, envy, and ambition of little men. They hoped to capitalize on sectional jealousies, fear of George Washington as a potential Cromwell, and distrust of France. But the dissidents never found a leader, never really came into the open. Any hope on their part that George Washington would resign was founded on a total misunderstanding of his character; to them his selfless dedication was incomprehensible. "I can assure you that no person ever heard me drop an expression that had a tendency to resignation," he wrote to the Rev. William Gordon in February 1778. " . . . to report a design of this kind is among the arts which those who are endeavoring to effect a change are practicing to bring it to pass. . . . While the public are satisfied with my endeavors I mean not to shrink in the cause, but the moment her voice, not that of faction, calls upon me to resign, I shall do it with as much pleasure as ever the weary traveller retired to rest."

If his companions in arms echoed the public voice, there was no danger of resignation. Their toast, wrote Mercy Warren to her husband, was "Washington or no army."

On The Home Front

Despite Cousin Lund's assurance that he would not desert his post, the subject of his continued service at Mount Vernon recurs from time to time in the correspondence between manager and employer. There was one contingency over which Lund had no control—a call to military service. In Virginia all ablebodied white males between the ages of sixteen and fifty were members of the militia, subject to service with their local units. A member of the militia might also be drawn by lot for service in a regiment raised to meet Virginia's quota of Continental troops. A man thus drawn was permitted to engage a substitute. On this topic General Washington wrote to Lund in February 1778, "If you should happen to draw a *prize* in the *militia*, I must provide a man, either there or here, inn your room: as nothing but your having the charge of my business, and the entire confidence I repose in you, could make me tolerable easy from home for such a length of time as I have been, and am likely to be." A few weeks later, 18 March, Lund responded:

The Court that presided over our draughting law in this County, was so exceedingly complisant [*sic*] they would not suffer me to take a chance for a prize. There was no law to exempt me, and they were sworn to do the work impartially. But I am thinking it will all be to do over again. The people murmer and say our draught was not agreeable to the letter of the law. In other Countys officers as well as men drew, here it was judged that it never was intended that the judges should judge themselves, therefore they did not draw. By which means one Colonel and two Captains (single men) took no chance for a prize. But a better reason will oblige them to draught again, the men who were draughted cannot be found.

It is apparent that if the drafting was repeated, Lund's exemption was continued. Although it may have been irregular, no reasonable person could have quarreled with it. George Washington's prolonged absence from Mount Vernon was "tolerable," as he expressed it, only by reason of Lund's continuing presence there.

Lund's statement that the men whose names had been drawn could not be found is indicative of the low state of public morale at this period. Inflation and the scarcity of many basic commodities were having their effect on many of those who had been most militant at the beginning of the war. Writing to his stepfather in June 1778, John Parke Custis noted that "the military ardor which displayed itself in Virginia in the beginning of this dispute in a distinguished manner, appears to be almost extinguished." In Loudoun County, which adjoins Fairfax, the draft provoked violent resistance. Evasion and organized opposition to military service were common throughout the state. Of an attempt to enlist volunteers in March 1778, Lund noted in a letter to his employer, "I have not been able to learn that more than 20 men within the State have as yet offered. That is twenty more than I expected." In this same letter he reported that in some counties men refused to accept service unless assured that General Washington would continue as commander-in-chief.

In a long letter dated 12 April 1778, the general's brother-in-law, Bartholomew Dandridge, confirmed the melancholy state of affairs in Virginia. On the subject of the draft he wrote, "I am afraid the Recruits for your army will not answer either your expectations or the occasion you will have for them. The law for drafting was very generally disliked and therefore badly executed, and from what I can learn instead of recruiting your Army with 2000 men will not furnish half the number." The accuracy of this prediction is confirmed by a headquarters return dated 23 May 1778, which reports that 716 draftees and substitutes had come in from Virginia. At the end of September the commander-in-chief, in a letter to an officer who was recruiting in Virginia, observed that his Virginia troops were "but a handful, compared to the Quota that they should furnish and unless something is done this handful will dwindle to nothing."

Virginia, the largest and by far the most populous of the newly independent states, was not unique in the feebleness of her war effort. These infant political communities, with a combined population of nearly three million, had the manpower, the material resources, and the overall capability to raise, equip, and provision the army for which the commander-in-chief so vainly pleaded—a trained and disciplined force which, under his leadership, could have overwhelmed that other George's uninspired hirelings. But new states do not come to maturity overnight, do not easily delegate control of their destinies to a distant and untried central government.

Nor could they bring themselves to demand of their constituents those sacrifices that must be made to underwrite the benefits so bravely proclaimed in the Declaration of Independence.

In consequence, the Continental army in the third winter of the war shivered, sickened, and starved at Valley Forge, while the Congress procrastinated and the several states busied themselves about their internal affairs. A well-fed civilian population warmed themselves at their cheerful hearths and slept in their own comfortable beds. At his headquarters George Washington labored to hold his dwindling army together, muted his defense against his critics lest he reveal the weakness of his position to the enemy and looked to Providence once again to come to his assistance.

In his letter of February 1778 to Lund, Washington wrote "I hope no motive, however powerful, will induce you to leave my business, whilst I, in a manner, am banished from home; because I should be unhappy to see it in common hands. For this reason, altho' from accidents and misfortunes not to be averted by human foresight, I make little or nothing from my Estate, I am still willing to increase your wages, and make it worth your while to continue with me." In his March letter previously quoted, Lund had replied: "By your letter I should suppose you were apprehensive I intended to leave you. I hope for the future you will entertain a better opinion of me than to believe that while you are encountering every danger and difficulty, at the hazard of your life and repose, giving up all domestic happiness, to serve the public and me among them, that I should attempt to take the advantage of you by screwing up my wages or leaving your estate to the care of a stranger." Apparently Lund was content with his wages. At any rate, he would not take advantage of his strong bargaining position. What these wages were does not appear, but in December of this same year General Washington reverted to the subject and stated that inflation had rendered them totally inadequate. He offered a share of current and future crops, the proportion to be determined by Lund. The

latter's election is not known. No doubt Lund's diffidence on
the subject of remuneration was based on the realization that
his employer was receiving no salary as commander-in-chief,
while he was playing a key civilian role at Mount Vernon in
lieu of military service. Loyalty to a cause and a family tie
demanded that he defer his ambition to own a place where he
could "give a neighbor beef and toddy."

Although Lund's local problems were many and complex,
they were not insoluble. The economy of that period was
simple, and in that simplicity there was strength to withstand
a long period of isolation. Lund's basic objective was self-sufficiency. Over and above that minimum goal, he must, if possible, find income to pay taxes, but the pressing necessity was
that the Mount Vernon community should feed, clothe, and
shelter itself. The prewar transition to crop diversification
and the well-developed domestic textile industry simplified
the solution of what might otherwise have been the most difficult of the basic problems. Shelter of a primitive but adequate kind could be provided by local workmen from materials close at hand. Fuel was always available from the woods
that constituted most of the estate acreage.

No topic recurs more frequently in Lund's letters to the
general than that of crops, always a newsworthy subject between men of the soil, and of increased importance during
this period. Crop news was usually discouraging. In December 1777, Lund reported that all of the wheat had been destroyed; the corn harvest had been short. Two months later
he wrote more optimistically; he would be able to sell "a
hundred or two barrels of common flour." In March 1778, he
reported a plan for curing 100 barrels of shad, to be sold for
the use of the army. Salt for curing the shad was to be provided by the government.

Fishing was an important activity at Mount Vernon in the
spring of the year, when shad and herring were running in
the Potomac. In 1774 Lund's account book records the sale of
more than 1000 barrels of fish. The catch during the war
years is not recorded, but it is apparent from Lund's corre-

spondence that it was limited by the shortage of salt for curing. Although by his own account Lund had over 300 bushels of salt at the beginning of the war, in March 1778 he was evaporating brine in which meat had been cured to recover the salt for reuse.

Writing to Lund in August 1778, General Washington sadly observed, "My Estate in Virginia is scarce able to support itself." The cause of this unhappy observation was another poor wheat crop, the third in as many years. Lund wrote that it was "worse if possible than any of the former," and remarked, "Surely there must be an end to the fly, as there is to the caterpillar, locust and many other insects." The fly that Lund blamed for his wheat losses was a "moth or fly weavil," which had appeared in North Carolina about forty years earlier and had moved slowly northward. It should not be confused with the "Hessian fly," which established itself in New England during the war and was equally destructive of wheat; this pest did not reach Virginia until after the war. Since wheat had been established at Mount Vernon as a principal crop, these continued failures were so discouraging that resumption of tobacco planting was considered. Whatever the decision may have been, the outlook was still gloomy in the spring of 1779, when General Washington acknowledged Lund's "melancholy account of your prospect for a crop." Although continuity of crop news is denied by the long break in Lund's letters, it is significant that in the last year of General Washington's absence, 1783, Lund wrote on the subject of crops, "We have not made a good one in my remembrance." Yet a survey of Lund's cash account reveals that his letters emphasized the darker side of the picture; his recorded receipts reflect a brighter aspect. Even the wheat crop that yielded so poorly afforded a surplus of flour for sale each year. There were also annual surpluses of corn and fish. Less regular but substantial income was realized from the sale of hay, mutton, beef, pork, bread (probably hard biscuit), wool, tallow, candles, and butter. Cattle on the hoof were also sold from annual increase. Some of these sales of commodities are noted "for the American Army." In 1781, when the allied forces moved on Yorktown, Lund sold seven oxen, eighty sheep, and a quantity of hay for the use of French troops who marched through Fairfax County. The ferry service that General Washington maintained from two of his Mount Vernon farms to opposite points on the Maryland shore contributed a small but regular revenue, and there were occasional stud fees.

In Lund's letters and account book there are references to several commodities that he considered manufacturing from raw materials at hand as a source of additional income. In 1775 he wrote to the general about saltpeter, for which there was a critical need in the production of powder. He elaborated on materials and methods of manufacture, but there is no evidence that he ever got the project under way. In 1776 he suggested the possibility of deriving molasses, sugar, and rum from cornstalks, using methods that had proven successful in Massachusetts. Corn as a major crop for this purpose he thought might be more remunerative than tobacco. The following summer he set up equipment for pressing the cornstalks and boiling down the juice, but he soon reported that the venture was a failure: "It will not quit the cost." In his cash account, under date of 6 July 1776, he noted a payment of one pound, ten shillings "To a Dutchman for Stayᵍ and instructing me six Days in the Art of Distillᵍ Whisky." If he practiced the art, it must have been on a small scale, for the refreshment of his restricted social circle only; there is no other reference to distilling in surviving sources. Whiskey was not a popular beverage at this period in Virginia. During the war distilling was discouraged to conserve grain; during part of the war years it was prohibited by act of legislature.

Lund's lack of proper bookkeeping method and the distorting effect of the wartime inflation combine to defeat analysis of his accounts. Hence, no statement of profit and loss can be adduced in evidence, but it can be affirmed that a high degree of self-sufficiency was attained, surpluses were marketed, and a program of improvements was carried to near completion, while no major deficits were incurred. More could scarcely have been asked under the circumstances.

MONMOUTH

Mrs. Washington left Valley Forge for Mount Vernon on
8 June 1778. She may have been escorted by Lund, who had
come to headquarters about the middle of May to confer with
his employer. John Parke Custis had intended to accompany
Lund to Valley Forge, but was diverted by his election to the
House of Burgesses for Fairfax County and journeyed southward to Richmond instead with George Mason of Gunston
Hall, his fellow delegate for Fairfax, to attend a meeting of
the legislature.

The departure of Mrs. Washington signaled the beginning
of the summer campaign. General Howe had resigned his
British command and returned to England. Sir Henry Clinton, his successor, was embarking his stores and baggage in
preparation for the evacuation of Philadelphia, his full intention as yet undisclosed. George Washington was under the
necessity of providing security for his own stores and for his
numerous invalids. His effective troops were put in a state of
instant readiness. When Clinton crossed the Delaware on the
early morning of 18 June with his long column headed toward
New York, the American army was marching on a paralleling
course within a matter of hours. On 28 June the two armies
met near Monmouth Court House. The outcome, General
Washington reported to his brother John Augustine on 4 July,
"from an unfortunate and bad beginning, turned out to be a
glorious and happy day." An American force of 5000 chosen
men under the command of Gen. Charles Lee had retreated
in disorder when the enemy was encountered. In his letter
the general discreetly withheld criticism. Lee was "in arrest,"
he wrote, "and a Court Martial sitting for tryal of him." A
"bountiful Providence" had enabled Washington to rally his
troops, make a stand, and recover the field. His report to John
Augustine was over-modest. One of his aides, Alexander
Hamilton, who was at his side in the heat of battle, wrote to
a friend:

America owes a great deal to General Washington for this days work. A general rout, dismay and disgrace would have attended the army in any other hands but his. By his own good sense and fortitude, he turned the fate of the day. Other officers have great merit in performing their parts well; but he directed the whole with the skill of a master workman. He did not hug himself at a distance, and leave an Arnold to win laurels for him [a reference to General Gates's conduct at Saratoga]; but by his own presence he brought order out of confusion, animated his troops, and led them to success.

Darkness brought an end to the battle; both sides were exhausted by the oppressive heat of the day. During the night the enemy silently stole away and accelerated their march to New York Bay.

From Monmouth the American army moved by easy stages to an earlier battlefield, White Plains. There General Washington wrote in retrospective vein to his friend Thomas Nelson of Virginia, "It is not a little pleasing, nor less wonderful to contemplate, that after two years of maneuvering and undergoing the strangest vicissitudes that perhaps ever attended any one contest since the creation both armies are brought back to the very point they set out from and, that that which was the offending party in the beginning is now reduced to the spade and pickaxe for defence." In all of this he again assigned a conspicuous part to Providence.

Gen. Charles Lee was convicted by the court martial on three counts, including disrespect to the commander-in-chief, and sentenced to be suspended from command for twelve months. Before the year was out he wrote an intemperate letter to Congress and was dismissed from the army. Lee had many admirers in high places, military and civilian. General Washington was impressed by his professional military background. In March 1776 he had described Lee in a letter to brother John Augustine as possessing an uncommon share of good sense, but noted that he was "rather fickle and violent I fear in his temper." His strange failure to recognize the man's unscrupulous ambition and latent treachery had near-fatal results at Monmouth. Fortunately, Providence was on the patriot side!

Monmouth was the last major engagement of the Revolution in the northern theater. The British and their tory auxiliaries continued to forage, plunder, and burn in vulnerable areas until the end of the war. As late as September 1781, an amphibious force under the command of the traitor Arnold attacked New London, Connecticut (Arnold's native state), massacred defending troops after they had surrendered, and systematically burned over 140 buildings in the town and a nearby hamlet. Such incidents served only to inflame passions and to strengthen patriot resistance.

FAMILY AFFAIRS AND A SOCIAL INTERLUDE

Some time in the late summer or early autumn of 1778 John Parke Custis made a deferred visit to headquarters. Custis was disposing of his inherited lands on the Eastern Shore of Virginia and in lower Tidewater. He needed his stepfather's signature releasing the dower interest of his mother and the general in these lands. At headquarters and by letter General Washington justified his own conduct in protecting this dower interest, at the same time earnestly advising against converting land, which had permanent value, into depreciating currency. Custis should not sell land, the general warned, until he had firm contracts to purchase equivalent acreage in the areas where he wished to reinvest. To Lund Washington the general confided in December 1778: "I am afraid Jack Custis, in spite of all the admonitions and advice I gave him against selling faster than he bought, is making a ruinous hand of his Estate."

The general's mother was also a source of continuing concern during his prolonged absence from home. In the early 1770s he had established her in Fredericksburg near her daughter, Betty Washington Lewis, himself taking over the management of Ferry Farm on the Rappahannock just below town, where she had been living. Before leaving Virginia he had instructed Lund Washington to meet all her calls for money. Lund's ledger records that he responded to her request on nine different occasions during the war. In one of her appeals to Lund, December 1778, Mrs. Washington wrote, "I never lived so pore in my life." It is evident that her complaints of poverty reached the ears of members of the Virginia legislature. In February 1781, Benjamin Harrison reported to the general that the lawmakers in Richmond had expressed a willingness to vote money for the relief of his mother. He replied immediately, asking that the matter be dropped, assuring Harrison that his mother had never complained of any inattention on the part of Lund. In truth, he wrote, she did not have a child who "would not divide the last sixpence to relieve her from any *real* distress . . . in fact she has an ample income of her own." Although this letter forestalled a pension or other public relief for his mother, her imagined privations continued to be a source of embarrassment to her children. In January 1783, the general wrote to brother John:

I learn from very good authority that she is upon all occasions and in all Companies complaining of the hardness of the times, of her wants and distresses; and if not in direct terms at least by strong innuendoes inviting favours which not only make *her* appear in an unfavourable point of view, but those who are connected with her. That she can have no *real* wants that may not be supplied I am sure of; imaginary wants are indefinite and oftentimes insatiable, because they are boundless, and always changing. The reason of my mentioning these matters to you now is that you may inquire into her real wants and see what is necessary to make her comfortable; . . . at the same time, I wish you to represent to her in delicate terms the impropriety of her complaints and acceptance of favours, even where they are voluntarily offered, from any but relations. It will not do to touch upon this subject in a letter to her, and therefore I have avoided it.

In the autumn of 1778, "Giving up all Idea this fourth Winter, of seeing my home and Friends, . . . " as he expressed it in a letter to John Augustine, the general invited Mrs. Washington to join him once again. On 11 November, in a letter to Col. John Mitchell, deputy quartermaster general in Philadelphia, he requested that replacement springs for Mrs. Washington's carriage be sent by special messenger to intercept her en route, south of Philadelphia. Mitchell was also asked to find lodgings for Mrs. Washington and stabling for her horses in the city.

On 22 December the general journeyed from his headquarters at Middle Brook, New Jersey, to Philadelphia, where he and Mrs. Washington lodged at the residence of Henry Laurens, member of Congress from South Carolina. The general had come to confer with the Congress. The season and the setting combined to encourage a continuous round of social activities. The residents of the City of Brotherly Love spared no effort to make this interlude agreeable to their distinguished guest, but, wrote General Greene to a fellow officer, "The exhibition was such a scene of luxury and profusion they gave him more pain than pleasure." His daily meetings with the Congress and its committees on numerous urgent problems of the hour, when contrasted with the social gaieties of the evenings, could only have deepened his melancholic forebodings. To his stepson he wrote on 2 January 1779: "You say, I shall be surprised at the slow progress made by your Assembly in the passage of bills through both houses. I really am not, nor shall I, I believe, be again surprised at anything; for it appears to me that idleness and dissipation seems to have taken such fast hold of everybody that I shall not be at all surprised if there should be a general wreck of everything."

APATHY AND INFLATION

It had been a matter of major concern to General Washington for some long time that the states separately were "too much engaged in their local concerns and have too many of their ablest men withdrawn from the general Council [Congress] for the good of the common weal," as he observed in a letter of 18 December 1778 to Benjamin Harrison. In a postscript to this letter under date of the thirtieth, he pressed this point, "I cannot help asking: Where is Mason, Wythe, Jefferson, Nicholas, Pendleton, Nelson, and another I could name." Where was his neighbor George Mason, author of the Fairfax Resolves, father of Virginia's Bill of Rights? Where was George Wythe, signer of the Declaration of Independence? Where was Thomas Jefferson, author of the Declaration? Where was Robert Carter Nicholas, a conservative patriot whose Williamsburg hospitality Washington had found so agreeable? Where was Edmund Pendleton, who with Patrick Henry had joined George Washington at Mount Vernon in the spring of 1774 and then journeyed on to Philadelphia with his fellow delegates to the First Continental Congress; who in 1776, as president of the Virginia Convention had drafted the resolve instructing Virginia's delegates in Congress to move for independence? Where was Thomas Nelson, who had carried the Convention's resolution to Philadelphia and as a member of Congress had signed the Declaration? Where was Benjamin Harrison, delegate to the First and Second Continental Congress and signer of the Declaration? Where were these fellow Virginians who in Williamsburg, at Mount Vernon, and in Philadelphia had joined him in moving from protest to petition and on to armed revolution? Could they not see that Virginia must send its best men to Congress, lest the common interest of America sink "into irretrievable ruin in which theirs also must be ultimately involved"?

By the autumn of 1778 depreciation of Continental currency had proceeded so far as to pose a question that General Washington phrased and answered in a 4 October letter to Gouverneur Morris: "Can we carry on the war much longer? Certainly *NO*, unless some measures can be devised and speedily exercised to restore the credit of our currency, restrain extortion and punish forestallers. Without these can be effected what funds can stand the present expenses of the

Army?" The situation, he thought, was one that would encourage Great Britain to prolong the war in hope of terms short of independence.

The entries in Lund Washington's Mount Vernon account book reflect this inflation. His record of cash receipts reveals that flour, which sold for fifteen shillings a hundredweight in 1776, was bringing ten pounds in 1779. During the same period salt pork had advanced from five to eighty pounds per barrel and corn from two shillings to eighty pounds per bushel. These figures are symptomatic of the financial distress that became increasingly acute and that was almost fatal to the patriot cause.

Congress had commenced the emission of bills of credit, or "Continental currency," in the summer of 1775, when it assumed the cost of supporting the troops about Boston and commenced planning for a Continental army. Lacking the power to tax, it had no recourse save drafts upon the states, and these were never effectively met. The states in turn were unwilling or unable to assess wartime expenses against the citizenry: they also turned to the printing press and commenced issuing their own paper money. These currencies were made legal tender and given a forced circulation by supporting regulations.

For the first year and a half inflation was not a significant factor and the impending evils were foreseen by few. One member of Congress is reported to have said: "Do you think, gentlemen, that I will consent to load my constituents with taxes when we can send to our printer and get a wagonload of money, one quire of which will pay for the whole?" As late as April 1779, Benjamin Franklin, who was then in France, wrote, "This currency, as we manage it, is a wonderful machine. It performs its office when we issue it; it pays and clothes troops and provides victuals and ammunition; and when we are obliged to issue a quantity excessive, it pays itself off by depreciation." Others, closer to the scene, were less sanguine. Richard Henry Lee, writing to Jefferson in 1779, complained that the annual rent on 4000 acres of land, fixed by prewar leases, would not buy twenty bushels of corn. George Washington felt the full effects of inflation officially and personally. On the personal side he was highly vulnerable, both as a landlord and as a creditor. Writing to Lund Washington late in 1778, he estimated that six or seven thousand pounds in bonds that he held were then worth as many hundred. In the spring of 1779 he confided to Burwell Bassett: "I am now receiving a Shilling in the pound in discharge of Bonds which ought to have been paid me, and would have been realized before I left Virginia, but for my indulgence to the debtors." A few months later he noted in a letter to another correspondent that rents on his lands in Berkeley County were not worth collecting. Here, ironically enough, was an inequity more painful than some of the mother country's taxes against which the colonists were contending, and probably no less offensive to George Washington's sense of justice. In August 1779, his strong feelings on the subject overflowed in a contradictory letter to Lund. He commenced by stating that after full consideration he was resolved to receive no more inflated currency in payment of old debts. He justified his position at length, but then said:

I wish you would consult Men of honor, honesty, and firm attachment to the cause, and govern yourself by their advice or by their conduct. If it be customary with others to receive money in this way, that is 6 d. or 1 / in the pound for old debts; if it is thought to be advansive of the great cause we are imbarked in for individuals to do so thereby ruining themselves while others are reaping the benefit of such distress. If the Law imposes this, and it is thought right to submit, I will not say aught against it, or oppose another word to it. No man has, nor no man will go further to serve the Public than myself, if sacrificing my whole Estate would effect any valuable purpose I would not hesitate one moment in doing it. But my submitting to matters of this kind unless it is done so by others, is no more than a drop in the bucket, in fact it is not serving the public but enriching individuals and countenancing dishonesty for sure I am that no honest Man would attempt to pay 20 / . with one or perhaps half a one. In a word I had rather make a present of the Bonds than receive payment of them in so shameful a way.

There is nothing in the surviving records to indicate whether Lund continued to accept inflated currency in payment of old debts.

George Washington's assertion that "no man has, nor no man will go further to serve the public than myself," was a plain statement of demonstrable fact. Despite his sense of injury by reason of wartime fiscal policy, he invested heavily in Loan Office certificates. These were the forerunners of our own Liberty Bonds and were sold at loan offices throughout the states. The record is fragmentary, but the inference is that Lund was instructed to invest all surplus funds in these securities and that more than fifty thousand dollars was so invested. Here also patriotism exacted a price, as the certificates were ultimately funded at less than 25 percent of face value. This little-known evidence of George Washington's unqualified devotion to the cause has inspired Dr. John Fitzpatrick to write in his *George Washington Himself* (p. 443) that, "If any other American of the Revolution backed the forlorn hope of independence with heart, mind, and purse as did George Washington, he is yet to be discovered."

In early February 1779, General Washington returned from Philadelphia to his Middle Brook headquarters, accompanied by Mrs. Washington. In a letter of 27 March to George Mason, he wrote with a freedom of expression based on his "unreserved friendship" with his Gunston neighbor. Each state he likened to a lesser part of a clock. How useless it was, he argued, to tend these parts while neglecting the great wheel and spring that must actuate and coordinate the whole mechanism. He had reason to believe, he wrote, that Britain a little while ago had resolved to negotiate peace, "upon almost any terms," but he feared that the present state of things would encourage her to continue the war. "Let this voice my dear Sir call upon you, Jefferson and others; do not from a mistaken opinion that we are about to set down under our own vine and fig tree let our hitherto noble struggle end in ignominy."

Life at headquarters during this fourth winter of the war

was now and again enlivened by social gatherings. On 18 February 1779 the first anniversary of the French alliance was celebrated by the artillery officers at General Knox's headquarters. There was a dinner, followed by a ball that lasted all night. In mid-March General Greene entertained at a dance at his quarters. On this occasion the commander-in-chief and Mrs. Greene are reported to have danced for three hours at a stretch. Heroes, we are reminded, should be men of great physical stamina. Early in June the general took to the field, and Mrs. Washington set out for Mount Vernon.

For three years Virginia had been free of war, but in early May 1779 a British force entered Chesapeake Bay, took possession of Portsmouth, and in the face of only feeble opposition, captured Suffolk. They sacked, burned, and looted—inflicting damage estimated at £2,000,000—and sailed away loaded with plunder, without the loss of a single man. "Riches so easily and cheaply purchased," General Washington wrote to brother John on 20 June, "will be a powerful inducement to another visit." About this time Richard Henry Lee wrote to Henry Laurens in Philadelphia from his home on the lower Potomac that tories from New York, in two large and eight small vessels, had burned warehouses in the neighborhood. Lee had led the local militia in defensive maneuvers.

In mid-October 1779, with little prospect of home leave, General Washington asked Colonel Mitchell to reserve "genteel" quarters in Philadelphia for Mrs. Washington, who was desirous of commencing her northward journey before the weather became severe and the roads bad. With quarters assured, she was invited to come on in early November. From Philadelphia she continued her northward journey, joining the general at Morristown soon after Christmas.

From Morristown on 18 March 1780, General Washington wrote to Lafayette that the oldest inhabitants "do not remember so hard a Winter as the one we are now emerging from. In a word the severity of the frost exceeded anything of the kind that had ever been experienced in this climate before." The suffering of the army in and about Morristown was fully as great as it had been at Valley Forge. Fortunately, the extreme cold and the depth of the snow hampered the British as severely as it did the patriot forces. In Virginia the winter was also unprecedented in severity. Of life at Mount Vernon during this period there is no record, but from other sources it is known that Chesapeake Bay was blocked by ice and that both pedestrian and wheeled traffic crossed Virginia and Maryland tidal rivers and creeks. Pedestrians also beat a path from Annapolis across the bay to the Eastern Shore, but normal traffic was at a standstill.

At the end of April 1780, the marquis de Lafayette returned from France, bringing word that a French expedition was on the way. A flotilla of warships and transports was bringing General Rochambeau with a force of five or six thousand troops. The immediate effect of this happy news was an aggravation of General Washington's problems. Already hard pressed to keep an army in being, he was now under the urgent necessity of raising a larger force for effective cooperation with these allies. Yet the prospect of French assistance so far had seemed only to deepen the prevailing state of lethargy. To cousin Lund at Mount Vernon he wrote on 19 May:

. . . new scenes are beginning to unfold themselves, which will by no means lessen my present trouble, or attention. You ask how I am to be rewarded for all this? There is one reward that nothing can deprive me of, and that is, the consciousness of having done my duty with the strictest rectitude, and most scrupulous exactness, and the certain knowledge, that if we should, ultimately, fail in the present contest, it is not owing to the want of exertion in me, or the application of every means that Congress and the United States, or the States individually, have put into my hands.

He acknowledged an indebtedness to Providence, adding, "The hour has now come when we stand much in need of another manifestation of its bounty however little we deserve it."

In a letter to John Augustine on 6 July he wrote:

In a word, we have no system, and seem determined not to profit by experience. We are, during the winter, dreaming of Independence and Peace, without using the means to become so. In the Spring when our Recruits should be with the Army and in training, we have just discovered the necessity of calling for them, and by the Fall, after a distresed, and inglorious campaign for want of them, we begin to get a few men, which come in just time enough to eat our Provisions, and consume our Stores without rendering any service; thus it is, one year Rolls over another, and with out some change, we are hastening to our Ruin.

For General Washington the unhappy winter had been followed by a second summer of military stalemate, a summer most memorable for Arnold's treason and his thwarted effort to deliver West Point to the enemy. Time and the wasted potential of a joint campaign with the French allies were running against the patriots. The commander-in-chief's letters to his Virginia friends became more urgent in their pleas for support. Congress had directed an inquiry into the conduct of General Gates at the disastrous battle of Camden and had authorized General Washington to appoint a new commander for the southern theatre. Washington chose Nathanael Greene and dispatched him promptly southward, bearing letters to men of influence in the governments of Virginia and the Carolinas. The Virginia letters were directed to George Mason, Archibald Carey, Benjamin Harrison, Edmund Pendleton, and Bartholomew Dandridge, the general's brother-in-law. All of the same date, 10 October 1780, they carried the same message, "We are without money, and have been so for a great length of time, without provisions and forage except what is taken by impress; without Cloathing; and shortly shall be (in a manner) without Men." If the war is to continue, he wrote, "there must be an entire new plan, government must undergo a reform, Congress must have power adequate to the purposes of the war." It would be difficult to determine the effect of these exhortations, which went by letter also to responsible men in the states to the northward, but their cumulative effect in the decisive months ahead should not be underestimated.

MOUNT VERNON HOSPITALITY

General Greene was accompanied southward by Baron Steuben, who had been assigned, under his command, to train and organize new units of the Continental army for duty in the southern theater. En route the two officers and their aides stopped at Mount Vernon, where Greene found time for a brief note to their commander:

Mount Vernon Nov. 13th, 1780

Sir

I arrived here just about noon, and met with a kind and hospitable reception by Mrs. Washington and all the family. Mrs. Washington, Mr. & Mrs. Custis (who are here) and Mr. Lund Washington and his Lady are all well.

We set out this morning for Richmond, and it is now so early that I am obliged to write by candle light. Nothing but the absolute necessity of being with my command as soon as possible should induce me to making my stay so short at your Excellency's seat; where there is every thing that nature and art can afford to render my stay happy and agreeable. Mount Vernon is one of the most pleasing places I ever saw; and I dont wonder that the glory of being commander in Chief, and the happiness of being universally admired could [not] compensate a person for such a sacrafice as you make. Baron Steuben is delighted with the place, and charmed with the reception we met here. Mrs. Washington sets out for camp about the middle of this week. . . .

Nath Greene

Baron Steuben was accompanied on this occasion by a young French aide, Pierre Etienne du Ponceau, who established himself in Pennsylvania after the war and became an American citizen. Fifty-seven years after his visit to Mount Vernon, in one of a series of letters to his granddaughter, he recalled his impressions of the occasion, quoting Steuben in more critical vein than did General Greene. The following excerpts are drawn from this letter:

On our way the Baron paid a visit to Mrs. Washington at Mount Vernon; we were most cordially received and invited to dinner.

The external appearance of the mansion did not strike the Baron very favorably. "If," he said, "Washington were not a better general than he was an architect the affairs of America would be in very bad condition." The house at the time might be considered handsome and perhaps elegant but at present the most that can be said of it is that it is a modest habitation, quite in keeping with the idea that we have of Cincinnatus, and of those of the other great commanders of the Roman Republic. Such is the idea that I formed of it at that time. In the interior we saw only two rooms separated by an entry, one of which was a parlour, the other the dining room. They were respectably but not luxuriously furnished.

The Baron having accepted the invitation we sat down to dinner. Mrs. Washington was accompanied by a young lady, a relative, whose name, I think, was Custis. The table was abundantly served, but without profusion. . . .

After dinner was over, while the Baron and Major Walker in company with the young lady were viewing the grounds I had the honour of sitting in the parlour tete-a-tete with Mrs. Washington. I shall never forget the affability, and, at the same time, the dignity of her demeanour. Our conversation was on general subjects. I can only remember the impression it left on my mind; she reminded me of the Roman matrons of whom I had read so much, and I thought that she well deserved to be the companion and friend of the greatest man of the age.

The inhabitants of the southern colonies are described by Nicholas Cresswell as:

. . . the most hospitable people on earth. If a stranger went amongst them, no matter of what country, if he behaved decently, had a good face, a good coat and a tolerable share of good nature, would dance with the women and drink with the men, with a little necessary adulation—of which, by the way, they are very fond— with these qualifications he would be entertained amongst them with the greatest friendship as long as he pleased to stay. If he is a traveller he is recommended from one Gentleman's house to another to his journey. I believe it possible to travel through both Carolinas, Virginia and Maryland without a single shilling, the Ferryages excepted. In short, there would be no fear of anything, but the constitution, which probably might suffer from the excess of good cheer.

A reading of George Washington's prewar diaries reveals a guest list that supports Cresswell's praise of southern hospitality. During a period of four months in 1773 the master's diary lists over one hundred friends, relatives, or respectable strangers who were guests at Mount Vernon, with their servants and their horses. All were wined and dined; most were lodged for at least one night. In that more leisurely age, a visit was easily prolonged by adverse weather or a polite invitation to linger. The war curtailed the accustomed social activities as men went off to the armies, but the war also generated traffic, and Mount Vernon was close enough to the main highways that converged at Alexandria to attract many travelers. One of these wartime wayfarers, George Grieve, translator and editor of Chastellux's *Travels in North America*, wrote:

The most perfect ease and comfort characterize the mode of receiving strangers in Virginia, but no where are these circumstances more conspicuous than at the house of General Washington. Your apartments are your home, the servants of the house are yours, and whilst every inducement is held out to bring you into the general society in the drawing room, or at the table, it rests with yourself to be served or not with every thing in your own chamber.

A brief passage in Lund's letter of 24 December 1777 to his employer touches upon this aspect of the local scene:

You Sir may think, (as every one would) that in your absence we live at a less expense than when you are at home, but it is the reverse. It is seldome that this house is without company. Our stables always full of horses . . . Custis keeps seven here; Mrs. Washington's charriot five, seven mares, the young horse that I cut in the fall (which I fear will never make more than a wagon horse), the wagon horses, and my one, making in the whole 24. These added to the visitors horses consume no small quantity of corn.

During Mrs. Washington's absences, Lund assumed a housekeeping responsibility that rested uncomfortably upon him. General Washington had anticipated the problem when he first sent for Mrs. Washington to join him in the autumn of 1775 and had offered a suggestion to which Lund responded: "In your letter you speak of Mrs. Barnes staying here in the absence of Mrs. Washington, to assist in taking care of the family. Mrs. Washington seems to think it will not answer. So that what to me is very disagreeable, I must encounter that of house keeping, but I will cheerfully do that and everything that lays in my power for you."

It would seem that Mrs. Washington's opinion was final in the domestic sphere. In this instance she may have had good reason for vetoing her husband's suggestion. Mrs. Barnes was the wife of a neighbor and probably a distant relative of the general on his mother's side, as her maiden name was Ball. She was an ambulatory character whose presence at Mount Vernon was frequently noted in the master's prewar diary, and his choice of words would indicate that she sometimes overstayed her welcome. On one occasion he noted while the lady was a guest that he "went to Mr. Barnes's upon Business of Mrs. Barnes and returned to Dinner." Apparently Mrs. Barnes was in frequent flight from an unhappy existence with her husband, and Mrs. Washington feared that with a little encouragement she might take permanent refuge under her roof. In any case her parting dictum left Lund with all the local responsibilities of both master and mistress. A few months later, 17 January 1776, he wrote unhappily: "I am by no means fit for a house keeper. I am afaid I shall consume more than ever, for I am not a judge how much should be given out every day. I am vexed when I am called upon to give out provisions for the day. God send you were both at home and an end to these troublesome times." In this same letter he confesses that he had fattened and slaughtered too many hogs and beeves: "You will ask me what we are going to do with so much meat. I cannot tell. When I put it up, I expected Mrs. Washington would have lived at home, if you did not, and was I to judge the future from the past consumption, there would have been a use for it—for I believe Mrs. Washington's charitable disposition increases in the same proportion as her meat house."

There are later references to Mrs. Washington's protegée, Milly Posey, daughter of an improvident former neighbor, that indicate Milly was at Mount Vernon for extended periods and assumed some household duties when in residence. In the autumn of 1779 Lund effected a more satisfactory solution of his problem by marrying. His bride was Elizabeth Foote, who, according to the most plausible interpretation of the genealogical data, was his first cousin and, like himself, was a third cousin of the general. Her diary and will establish that Betsey, as the family called her, was remarkable for her extreme piety. She was installed in the mansion and there resided with her husband for the remainder of the war.

YEAR OF DECISION

The year 1781 culminated so gloriously for the American cause at Yorktown as to dim the memory of the gloom that had prevailed a few months earlier. When Congress sent young John Laurens, General Washington's military aide, to France to plead the urgent need of the states for aid, Laurens carried General Washington's solemn warning (letter of 15 January) that without a substantial loan, "we may make a feeble and expiring effort the next campaign." Naval superiority on the American coast was most important, he wrote; additional French troops "would be extremely desirable." Faith in the French ally was waning. Some believed that France saw an advantage to herself in allowing Britain and her former colonies to exhaust themselves further in a prolonged struggle.

Morale in Virginia reflected the symptoms common to all the states. When at the opening of the new year a hostile fleet entered Hampton Roads, it was virtually unopposed. The expedition, with the hated traitor Benedict Arnold at the head of land forces, moved up the James River and, on 5 January occupied Richmond. Having destroyed public stores and plundered the town, the enemy returned downriver to Portsmouth without having encountered any effective opposition. In March, Arnold was replaced by a new commander, and an augmented British force moved up the James once again. This time Petersburg was occupied and became a base of operations from which destructive raids were launched into the country roundabout.

Tidewater Virginia, thinly populated and deeply indented by Chesapeake Bay and its tributary navigable rivers, was peculiarly vulnerable to waterborne attack. Although the state maintained a small navy and every ablebodied citizen was a member of the militia, the combined efforts of her naval and land forces were never able to give adequate protection to her shores. More feared than British naval vessels were the "picaroons," small craft manned by professed loyalists. General Washington referred to these marauders as "a lawless Banditti who would rob both sides with equal impunity." These partisans were particularly active in the spring of 1781. On 24 April, Fielding Lewis, Washington's brother-in-law, writing to the general from Fredericksburg, reported:

The enemy's privateers are troublesome on the rivers, no person who lives on the banks of the Potomac can have any certainty of not being taken out of his bed before morning. Most people have removed their furniture, and many families are gone into the forest where places could be got. Col. J. Washington has removed to his son in Laws Mr. W. Washington's near Popes Creek. I expect he

A LETTER FROM THE GENERAL TO COUSIN LUND
IS INTERCEPTED BY THE ENEMY

Fig. 23. During the Revolution most of General Washington's letters to his wife and manager at Mount Vernon, as well as his private correspondence with other family and friends in Virginia, was entrusted to the public post, which was, at best, a precarious means of conveyance. Privacy was not assured, and capture of a postrider by a British military patrol was always a possibility, as is evidenced by this partial publication in Rivington's *Gazette* (New York), 4 April 1781, of the general's 28 March letter to Lund. The obvious purpose of this publication was to embarrass the American commander in his relations with the French allies. General Rochambeau's amiable acknowledgement of Washington's letter of explanation and apology assured that the alliance was not weakened by his friend's indiscreet comments.
(From a copy at the Library of Congress.)   *(overleaf)*

On Saturday another Rebel Mail was brought to this City, taken last Thursday, with Montaigne the Post Rider, who was in person brought to town by the captors. It contained a great number of letters in the bags from New England, Rhode Island, Connecticut, Fish-Kill, New Windsor, &c.—The Public may depend on the genuineness of the following Letter.

———To Mr. Lund Washington, at Mount Vernon, Virginia.

" *New Windsor, March* 28, 1781.

" *Dear Lund,*

" SINCE my last your letter of the 14th inst. is received. If Mr. Triplet has got as much land as he has given, and you have paid him the cash difference, with a proper allowance for the depreciation since the bargain was made, I am at a loss to discover the ground of his complaint—and if men will complain without cause, it is a matter of no great moment.--It always was, and now is my wish to do him justice, and if there is any thing lacking in it, delay not to give full measure of justice, because I had rather exceed than fall short.

" We have heard nothing certain of the two fleets since they left their respective ports.----We wait with impatient anxiety for advices from Chesapeak, and the southern army-----God send they may be favourable to us.----A detachment from New - York has made two or three attempts to put to

cun-
oncur
guns,
r.g te
sithde
d his,
. Ro-
l dif-
h p-

ßand
roops
backs
rize;
forces
Vir-
Bant
ning
great
Ad-
un-
tóber
a, or

fleet
n of
con-

uth-
t nt,
, at
That
with
uber
e a-
lla's
We
this

the
h of
ilec
As.

sea (for the purpofe, it is faid, of re-
inforcing either Arnold or Cornwallis)
and as often returned----My laft accounts from New-York mention another attempt on the 25th, but whether
with truth, or not, it is not in my
power to fay.----It was unfortunate----
but this I mention in confidence---that
the French fleet and detachment did
not undertake the enterprize they are
now upon, when I firft propofed it to
them.----The deftruction of Arnold's
corps would then have been inevitable
before the Britifh fleet could have been
in a condition to put to fea.   Inftead
of this the fmall fquadron, which took
the Romulus and other veffels, was
fent, and could not, as I foretold, do
any thing without a land force at Porti-
mouth.   I am
   Your affectionate friend and fervant,
            G. WASHINGTON."

Theatre.

Monday next, the 9th inftant, will be
prefented a TRAGEDY (never
performed here) called

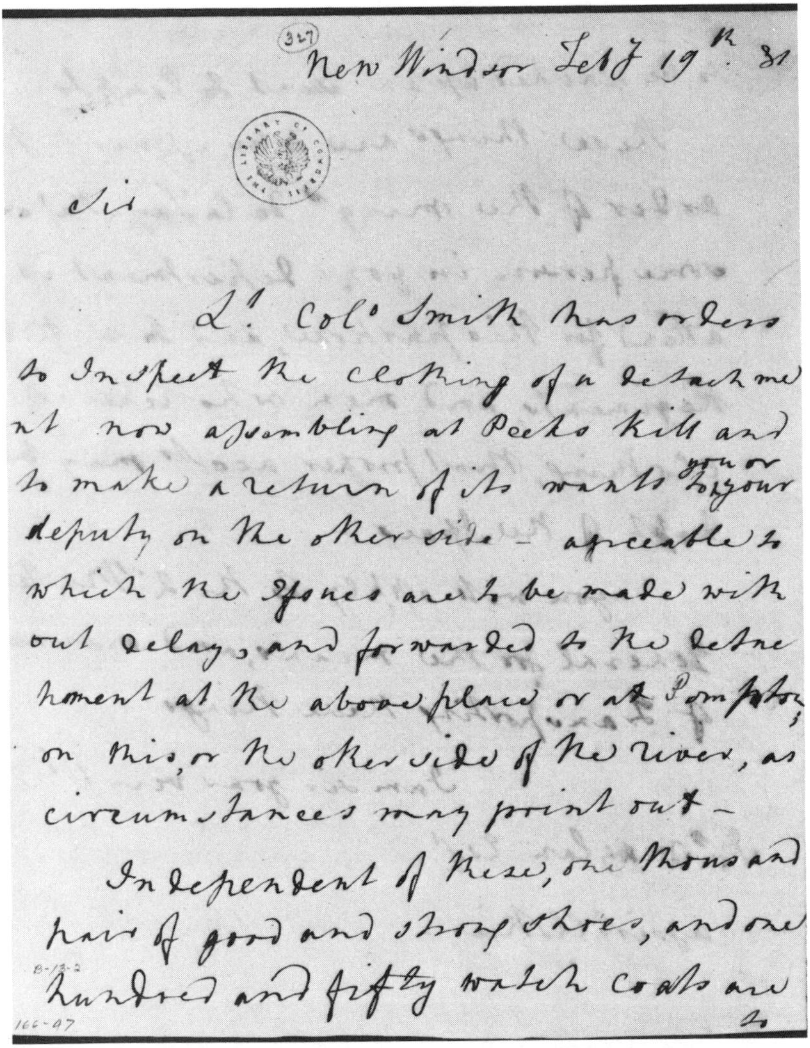

New Windsor Feby 19th. 81

Sir

Lt. Col. Smith has orders to Inspect the clothing of a detachment now assembling at Peeks kill and to make a return of its wants to your deputy on the other side — agreeable to which the Issues are to be made without delay, and forwarded to the detachment at the above place or at Pompton; on this, or the other side of the river, as circumstances may point out —

In dependent of these, one thousand pair of good and strong shoes, and one hundred and fifty watch coats are

MARTHA WASHINGTON, CLERK-COPYIST

Fig. 24. In the course of her sojourns at the winter quarters of the army, Mrs. Washington was occasionally pressed into clerical service, as evidenced by this first page of a two-page retained copy, in her hand, of General Washington's letter to John Moylan, assistant army clothier, from headquarters, New Windsor, New York, 19 February 1781.
(Reproduced from the collection of the Library of Congress.)

has given you better information about the matter than I am able; our distress is truly alarming no arms to defend ourselves.

In a postscript he noted a report that the British were moving up the James; the inhabitants of Richmond were removing public stores and private property. The impending meeting of the assembly, he thought, would be held in Fredericksburg or Alexandria.

On 12 April Alexandria had been alarmed by the approach of six armed vessels, but Col. John Fitzgerald, a citizen of the town and veteran of several years' service as aide to General Washington, made such a show of force that the vessels retreated. Two weeks later Lafayette (See figs. 25 and 26), en route southward with a small detachment of Continentals to oppose the British forces in Virginia, learned of an incident that had occurred at Mount Vernon on this occasion. Following is his report of the incident to his commander:

Alexandria April 23d 1781

My Dear General

Great happiness is derived from friendship, and I do particularly experience it in the attachment which unites me to you. But friendship has its duties, and the man that likes you the best will be the forwardest in letting you know every thing where you can be concerned.

When the enemy came to your house many Negroes deserted to them. This piece of news did not affect me much as I little value those concerns, but you cannot conceive how unhappy I have been to hear that Mr. Lund Washington went on board the enemy's vessels and consented to give them provisions. This being done by the gentleman who in some measure represents you at your house will certainly have a bad effect, and contrasts with spirited answers from some neighbours that had their houses burnt accordingly.

You will do what you think proper about it, my dear General, but, as your friend, it was my duty *confidentially* to mention the circumstances. . . .

My dear General

Your most obe^nt servant and friend

Lafayette

THE MARQUIS DE LAFAYETTE

Fig. 25. This portrait by Charles Willson Peale was commissioned by General Washington in 1779 and hung at Mount Vernon until the death of Mrs. Washington, when it passed to her grandson, George Washington Parke Custis.
(From the Collection of Washington and Lee University, Lexington, Virginia.)

The Main Key of the Fortress of Despotism

Fig. 26. The key of the Bastille was so identified by General Lafayette in his accommpanying letter of presentation to General Washington. The gift, he wrote, was "a tribute, which I owe as a son to my adoptive father, as an aide-de-camp to my general, as a missionary of liberty to its patriarch" (Paris, 17 March 1790). Key and case were relinquished to the association by the general's great-grandnephew, John Augustine Washington III, last private owner of Mount Vernon, in 1859. The framed sketch of the prison in process of demolition, here illustrated, replaces the original, which was sold at auction by descendants of Washington's heirs. It was reproduced from an illustration in the auction catalogue.
(Courtesy of the Mount Vernon Ladies' Association.)

In acknowledgment General Washington wrote:

New Windsor, May 4, 1781

My dear Marquis: The freedom of your communications is an evidence to me of the sincerety of your attachment; and every fresh instance of this gives pleasure and adds strength to the band which unites us in friendship. In this light I view the intimation contained in your letter of the 23d. Ulto., from Alexandria, respecting the conduct of Mr. Lund Washington.

Some days previous to the receipt of your letter, which only came to my hands yesterday; I received an acct. of this transaction from the Gentn. himself, and immediately wrote, and forwarded, the answer of which the inclosed is a copy. this Letter, which was written in the moment of my obtaining the first intimation of the matter may be considered as a testimony of my disapprobatn. of his conduct; and the transmission of it to you as a proof of my friendship; because I wish you to be assured that no man can condemn the measure more sincerely than I do.

A false idea, arising from the consideration of his being my Steward and in that character was more the trustee and guardian of my property than the representative of my honor has misled his judgment and plunged him into error (upon the appearance of desertion in my Negros, and danger to my buildings) for sure I am, that no man is more firmly opposed to the enemy than he. From a thorough conviction of this, and of his integrity I entrusted every species of my property to his care; without reservation, or fear of his abusing it.

The last paragraph of my letter to him was occasioned by an expression of his fear, that all the Estates convenient to the river would be stripped of their Negros and moveable property. . . .

Mrs. Washington and the rest of my (small) family which at present consists only of Tilghman and Humphrey join me in cordial salutations, and with sentiments of the purest esteem etc.

His letter to Lund, of which he enclosed a copy to Lafayette, reads as follows:

New Windsor, April 30, 1781

Dear Lund: Your letter of the 18th came to me by the last Post. I am very sorry to hear of your loss; I am a little sorry to hear of my own; but that which gives me most concern, is that you should go on board the enemys Vessels, and furnish them with refreshments. It would have been a less painful circumstance to me, to have heard, that in consequence of your non-compliance with their request, they had burnt my House, and laid the Plantation in ruins. You ought to have considered yourself as my representative, and should have reflected on the bad example of communicating with the enemy, and making a voluntary offer of refreshments to them with a view to prevent a conflagration.

It was not in your power, I acknowledge, to prevent them from sending a flag on shore, and you did right to meet it; but you should, in the same instant that the business of it was unfolded, have declared, explicitly, that it was improper for you to yield to the request; after which, if they had proceeded to help themselves, *by force*, you could have submitted (and being unprovided for defence) this was to be prefered to a feeble opposition which only serves as a pretext to burn and destroy.

I am thoroughly perswaded that you acted from your best judgment; and believe, that your desire to preserve my property, and rescue the buildings from impending danger, were your governing motives. But to go on board their Vessels; carry them refreshments; commune with a parcel of plundering Scoundrels, and request a favor by asking the surrender of my Negroes, was exceedingly ill-judged, and 'tis to be feared, will be unhappy in its consequences, as it will be a precedent for others, and may become a subject of animadversion.

I have no doubt of the enemys intention to prosecute the plundering plan they have begun. And, unless a stop can be put to it by the arrival of a superior naval force, I have as little doubt of its ending in the loss of all my Negroes, and in the destruction of my Houses; but I am prepared for the event, under the prospect of which, if you could deposit, in safety, at some convenient distance from the Water, the most valuable and least bulky articles, it might be consistent with policy and prudence, and a mean of preserving them for use hereafter. Such, and so many things as are necessary for common, and present use must be retained and run their chance through the firy trial of his summer.

Mrs. Washington joins me in best and affectionate regard for you, Mrs. Washington and Milly Posey; and does most sincerely regret your loss. I do not know what Negros they may have left you; and as I have observed before, I do not know what number they will have left me by the time they have done; but this I am sure of, that you shall never want assistance, while it is in my power to afford it. I am etc.

Lund's letter of 18 April to General Washington does not survive, but the translator of Chastellux's *Travels in North America*, George Grieve, reports Lund's version of the affair in a footnote to that publication, as follows:

Mr. Lund Washington, a relation of the General's, and who managed all his affairs during his nine years absence with the army, informed me that an English frigate having come up the Potomac, a party was landed who set fire to and destroyed some gentlemen's houses on the Maryland side in sight of Mount Vernon, the General's house, after which the Captain (I think Captain Graves of the Actaeon) sent a boat on shore to the General's, demanding a large supply of provisions, &c. with a menace of burning it likewise in case of a refusal. To this message Mr. Lund Washington replied, "That when the General engaged in the contest he had put all to stake, and was well aware of the exposed situation of his home and property, in consequence of which he had given him orders by no means to comply with any such demands, for that he would make no unworthy compromise with the enemy, and was ready to meet the fate of his neighbours." The Captain was highly incensed on receiving this answer, and removed his frigate to the Virginia shore; but before he commenced his operations, he sent another message to the same purport, offering likewise a passport to Mr. Washington to come on board; he returned accordingly in the boat, carrying with him a small present of poultry, of which he begged the Captain's acceptance. His presence produced the best effect, he was hospitably received, notwithstanding he repeated the same sentiments with the same firmness. The Captain expressed his personal respect for the character of the General, commending the conduct of Mr. Lund Washington, and assured him nothing but his having misconceived the terms of the first answer could have induced him for a moment to entertain the idea of taking the smallest measure offensive to so illustrious a character as the General, explaining at the same time the real or supposed provocations which had compelled his severity on the other side of the river. Mr. Washington, after spending some time in perfect harmony on board, returned, and instantly dispatched sheep, hogs, and an abundant supply of other articles as a present to the English frigate.

This account by Grieve does not mention the six small vessels that menaced Alexandria; perhaps they were auxiliaries of the larger craft. George Mason, who was unmolested, reported that there were "several enemy ships." Henry Lee of Leesylvania, a few miles below Gunston, identified the force as "several schooners." Nor does Grieve's friendly narration of the event excuse Lund's conduct; General Washington's reprimand was well deserved. His loss is recorded as "A very valuable Boat: 24 foot Keel," and eighteen slaves, seven of whom were later recovered. Lund's loss is not noted. His indiscretion may have saved Mount Vernon, but it is permissable to accept at face value the captain's reported statement that his personal respect for General Washington saved his home from destruction on this occasion.

In May Cornwallis marched his army northward into Virginia, joining the force at Petersburg on the nineteenth. Confronted by this formidable combination, Lafayette adopted evasive tactics. When the British army moved northward, he retreated beyond Fredericksburg. It was at this juncture that Cornwallis is said to have remarked, "The boy cannot escape me." The Mount Vernon neighborhood felt the menace of his advance. George Mason sent his movable effects across the Potomac and prepared to follow with his family. But Cornwallis paused and sent detachments westward. The wonder is that Fredericksburg, with its busy munitions manufactory, was bypassed. In January Fielding Lewis's associate in that enterprise, Maj. Charles Dick, had reported to Governor Jefferson that "the gentlemen of this town and even the Ladys have very spiritedly attended at the Gunnery and assisted to make up already 20,000 cartridges with bullets from which the Spottsylvania Militia and also from Caroline have been supplied, as also above 100 guns from the Factory."

On 28 May Governor Jefferson wrote to General Washington urging his presence in Virginia: "Your appearance among them [his fellow Virginians] would restore full confidence of salvation, and would render them equal to whatever is not impossible. . . . The difficulty would then be how to keep men out of the field." A few days after this letter was written, Jefferson and his family fled from Monticello on the approach of a unit of Tarleton's cavalry, narrowly escaping capture.

Monticello was spared, as Mount Vernon had been a short time before, but Jefferson's plantation Elk Hill, on the James River between Charlottesville and Richmond, was not so fortunate. Here, where Cornwallis made his headquarters for ten days, growing crops were destroyed and barns and their contents were burned. Cattle, sheep, and hogs were slaughtered for the subsistence of his troops. The serviceable horses were requisitioned; the rest were slaughtered. All of the fences on the plantation were burned.

Chastellux in his *Travels* records a vivid account by a tavern keeper in New Kent County, east of Richmond, of the plundering as Cornwallis withdrew eastward toward the bay:

It was comparatively nothing to see fruit, fowl, and cattle carried away by the light troops which formed the vanguard, to see the army gather up what the vanguard had left, and even the officers seize the rum and all kinds of provisions without paying a farthing for them. This hurricane, which destroyed everything in its path, was followed by a scourge yet more terrible: a numerous rabble, under the names of Refugees and Loyalists, followed the army, not to assist in the field, but to share the plunder. The furniture and clothing of the inhabitants was in general the only booty left to satisfy their avidity; after they had emptied the houses, they stripped the owners; and Mr. Byrd still recalled with distress that they had forcibly taken the very boots off his feet.

In justice to the British it must be noted that an effort was made to protect the civilian population from insult and violence. Dr. Robert Honyman notes in his journal that in this same neighborhood two soldiers who had ravished a nine-year-old girl were given a summary trial before Colonel Simcoe, one of Cornwallis's lieutenants, and were hanged in the presence of the whole army.

Mount Vernon survived the "Firy trial" of the summer (as General Washington termed it) without further molestation, and there is no mention in local annals of the presence of British men-of-war or picaroons on the upper Potomac during the remainder of the war. The ominous course of events in Virginia during the spring and early summer caused Mrs. Washington to postpone her return to Mount Vernon. She left headquarters at New Windsor "in a very low and weak state," the general wrote, "having been sick for more than a month with a kind of Jaundice." She stopped in Philadelphia, where she remained until hostilities had localized in the area east of Richmond. She reached home about 1 August.

On 14 August, at his headquarters on the Hudson, the commander-in-chief noted in his diary that matters had "come to a crisis." He had just received a dispatch from the count de Barras at Newport reporting that the count de Grasse was about to sail from San Domingo to Chesapeake Bay with a fleet of from twenty-five to twenty-nine ships of the line and 3200 troops. Washington's joint plan with Rochambeau for an attack on New York must be put aside. The naval superiority for which he had so long hoped was about to materialize in the Chesapeake; a new plan must be adopted. Barras must be persuaded to join de Grasse in the Chesapeake with his small fleet, bringing salt, provisions, rum, and seige guns. A detachment of Continentals and the French force under Rochambeau, which were encamped about Dobbs Ferry, must move southward with all possible speed to cooperate with de Grasse and the troops under Lafayette in opposing Cornwallis. General Rochambeau, under instruction to regard General Washington as his superior officer, was completely cooperative. The French admirals, being under no such directive, were less dependable. De Grasse had written that he must return to the West Indies by mid-October. On the sixteenth a courier brought news that Cornwallis was entrenching at Yorktown and Gloucester; time was of the essence. By 19 August the American and French forces were on the march. They were well advanced toward Philadelphia before Clinton in New York was aware of the change in plans. In Philadelphia on 1 September Washington learned that a British fleet of twenty ships of the line had sailed from New York for an undisclosed destination. To Lafayette he wrote, "I am almost all impatience and anxiety." His Continentals, ill-clothed and long unpaid, were reluctant to go forward. At Washington's urging and by a desperate effort, Robert Morris raised $20,000 in specie to be distributed among them. At Chester a courier brought word that de Grasse was in the bay; in a moment of exultation Washington embraced Rochambeau. While the troops were embarking at the head of the bay, the generals rode on toward Baltimore with their staffs. For the American general the pace was too slow. With a single aide he forged ahead, covering the one hundred and twenty miles to Mount Vernon in two days. The aide, David Humphreys, had been hard pressed to keep up.

More than six years had passed since the master of Mount Vernon had left home on a morning in early May of 1775 to attend the Continental Congress in Philadelphia. It was a happy moment, but there was no time for reflection and little leisure for inspection of the structural transformations that had been carried forward under Lund's supervision. There is no record of a meeting with Mrs. Washington's four young grandchildren—Eliza Parke Custis, age 5 years; Martha, 4 years; Eleanor, 2½ years; and their young brother, George Washington Parke Custis, age 6 months—whose parents had settled at Abingdon, just above Alexandria, where today a portion of an end wall and chimney base of their home overlooks the runways of National Airport. These young children must certainly have been brought to Mount Vernon to be presented to their illustrious stepgrandfather.

The morning after his arrival General Washington dispatched a hurried note to Lafayette:

We are thus far, My Dear Marquis, on our way to you. The Count de Rochambeau has just arrived, General Chattelux will be here, and we propose (after resting tomorrow) to be at Fredericksburg on the night of the 12th; the 13th we shall reach New Castle, and the next day we expect the pleasure of seeing you at your Encampment.

Should there be any danger as we approach you, I shall be obliged if you will send a party of Horse towards New Kent Court House to meet us. With great personal regd. etc.

P.S. I hope you will keep Lord Cornwallis safe, without Provisions or Forage untill we arrive. Adieu.

A letter was dispatched to Peter Waggoner, neighbor, friend, and former fox-hunting companion, who was now a colonel in command of the local militia. Army wagons, cattle on the hoof, and cavalry were on the way; the road through Fairfax County must be repaired. Colonel Hendricks, deputy quartermaster general in Alexandria, was instructed to improve the approaches to the ferry across the Potomoc at Georgetown. There were letters also to General Weedon, General Lincoln, and the governor of Maryland on matters of military moment. The brevity of Washington's own diary notation of this stopover is indicative of his haste and his preoccupation with events at a distance: "I reached my own Seat at Mount Vernon (distant 110 Miles from the Hd. of Elk) where I staid till the 12th. and in three days afterwards that is on the 15th. reached Williamsburg." Brief entries in the journal of Col. J. Trumbull, Jr., one of the general's military aides, add little to the surviving record of this high moment in the history of Mount Vernon:

10. Arrive at Mount Vernon just as the family are at dinner. Count Rochambeau arrives at evening.
11th. At Mount Vernon General Chastilux arrives with his aids. A numerous family now present. All accommodated. An elegant seat and situation, great appearance of oppulence and real exhibitions of hospitality & princely entertainment.

In her biography of George Mason, Kate Mason Rowland reports that there was a dinner party at Mount Vernon on the eleventh, but she offers no details. Perhaps Mason and other neighbors were invited to meet and dine with the distinguished guests. If not, these gentlemen with their aides would have composed an impressive dinner party even without reinforcement.

On the morning of the twelfth the general and his guests resumed their journey. Servants had been sent ahead at daybreak to arrange for forage for the horses and accomodations at Fredericksburg's best tavern for the travelers. General

Weedon had been requested to engage carriages to ease the journey of the French, or fresh horses if carriages were not available. Before the party reached Fredericksburg a rider with dispatches for Congress was encountered. The man reported that de Grasse had taken his fleet to sea to engage the British and had disappeared with them. The potentialities were dismaying. Orders were dispatched halting the movement of the troop-laden boats down the bay. Not until the night of 14/15 September in Williamsburg was the anxiety relieved. De Grasse reported his return to the bay with two captured frigates after a favorable engagement with the British fleet, which returned in diminished and crippled state to New York. Barras's squadron, with its guns and provisions, had joined de Grasse. Naval supremacy was assured; the troops so long afloat from the head of the bay could proceed. Cornwallis's fate was sealed!

On 12 October John Parke Custis wrote to his mother from the headquarters of the American army before Yorktown, where he was acting as a volunteer aide to the commander-in-chief without rank or pay. This letter, perhaps the last he wrote, is in the Mount Vernon collection. The text follows:

Camp before York October 12th 1781

My Dear & Hon^d. Madam

I have the pleasure to inform you that I find myself much better since I left Mt. Vernon, notwithstanding the change in my Lodging &c. and that the General tho in constant Fatigue looks very well; I staid a Night with my Uncle in my way down, and had the pleasure to find him and Family in good Health. Likewise of seeing my Grandmother, I think She looks very well, but discovers her great age more than when I last saw Her. She now lives with my Uncle. My Aunt Henley lives where she formerly lived. They are all very desirous of seeing You, My Grandmother wishes You to bring down both Bet and Pat, but I told Her it would be to inconvenient for you to bring down both. my Uncle has suffered very much by the Enemy. They are all very desirous of seeing you, and if the General has no Objections, I think you might come down; as he is writing to you, I shall refer you to him for advise on this Matter as well as for News.

> I am my dear Madam with
> the sincerest Affection Your
> very dutiful son

J.P. Custis
P.S. Please to inform M^r. Washington that I have made every possible Enquiry after his Negroes, but have not seen any belonging to him the General or myself. I have heard that Ned is in York a pioneer. Old Doc Cachier [Pachier?] is in this Neighbourhood tho I have not been able to see him. his Wife is dead and I fear that most who left us are not existing. The Mortality that has taken place among the wretches is really incredible. I have seen numbers lying dead in the Woods, and many so exhausted they cannot walk. I should be glad to hear from M^r. W——n whether he has sold any of my horses. they are not high priced in comparison to what they sell for here—

JPC

The uncle mentioned by Custis was probably his mother's brother, Bartholomew Dandrige, although it might have been her brother-in-law Burwell Bassett of Eltham. The grandmother was Mrs. Washington's mother, Mrs. John Dandridge. Bet and Pat were Custis's two older daughters, Eliza and Martha. The Negroes referred to in the postscript would have been those taken from Mount Vernon in April. By contemporary estimate, British forces in 1781 carried away 30,000 Virginia Negroes, nine-tenths of whom died of starvation or epidemic disease.

A few days after writing this letter Custis was stricken with camp fever. It is traditional that he remained at Yorktown by his own desire to witness the surrender ceremony on the nineteenth. He was then taken to Eltham; Dr. Craik may have been in attendance. Accounts of Custis's fatal illness and death, written many years after the event, are interwoven with much that is circumstantial and contradictory. General Washington's letter of 6 November to Colonel Trumbull is the only contemporary document in evidence:

Eltham, November 6, 1781

Colo. Bassets.

My dear Sir: I came here in time to see Mr. Custis breathe his last. About Eight o'clock yesterday Evening he expired. The deep and solumn distress of the Mother, and affliction of the Wife of this amiable young Man, requires every comfort in my power to afford them; the last rights of the deceased I must also see performed; these will take me three or four days; when I shall proceed with Mrs. Washington and Mrs. Custis to Mount Vernon.

As the dirty tavern you are now at cannot be very comfortable; and in spite of Mr. Sterne's observation the House of Mourning not very agreeable; it is my wish, that all of the Gentn of my family, except yourself, who I beg may come here and remain with me; may proceed on at their leizure to Mount Vernon, and wait for me there. Colo. Cobb will join you on the road at the Tavern we breakfasted at (this side Ruffens). My best wishes attend the Gentn. and with much sincerity and affectn. I remain, etc.

The death of John Parke Custis at the age of twenty-seven was a tragic event for his family. His mother was now childless, having survived the four children of her first marriage— the two who had died in infancy, Patsy, who had died of epilepsy just before the war, and now her adored Jackie. Many years later his oldest daughter noted in a long autobiographical letter that at the beginning of the war, "he was ready to fly to arms and wished to follow Washington to battle—but the Prayers of his Mother, the entreaties and caresses of his Wife, had power to alter his determination." And now at the moment of what might well prove to have been the successful military culmination of the war, he was gone, a noncombatant casualty, leaving four young children and an involved estate. His stepfather had been critical of his management of his affairs, but the feeling was that of a concerned parent. In the words of a contemporary, he was "uncommonly affected at his death. . . . It is certain that they were upon terms of the most affectionate and manly friendship." The fact that young Custis was one of Fairfax County's two representatives in the General Assembly is an evidence of the high regard in which he was held by his neighbors.

As soon as the funeral offices at Eltham were completed,

the general turned northward with Mrs. Washington, the widowed daughter-in-law, and little "Bet," her five year old. Trumbull rode with them; his account of official expenses is the only record of this melancholy journey over a route that had become familiar to the general and his lady since they had first followed it together on their wedding journey from Williamsburg to Mount Vernon in the spring of 1759.

A plaintive note from Mary Washington to her son some time later expresses her regret that she was not at home when he passed through Fredericksburg. Here—if there had been no opportunity in his hurried passage southward some weeks earlier, as seems likely—Washington would have called on his sister and brother-in-law, the Fielding Lewises, at Kenmore. This would have been another somber occasion, a final farewell to Lewis, who had been in ill health for over a year. He died some time between 10 December, when he added a codicil to his will, and 17 January 1782, when the document was filed for probate. As chief commissioner of a small-arms manufactory that has been established in Fredericksburg by the General Assembly at the beginning of the war, Colonel Lewis had advanced his own funds when public money fell short of need. He died leaving his family in straitened circumstances.

Back at Mount Vernon once again for a brief interval, the master found many matters great and small competing for his attention. Most prominent and of compelling interest were the structural improvements. These, we may be certain, were closely inspected with Lund, and plans for their completion would have been discussed. The many aspects of local husbandry would have been a subject of lengthy discussions also, as time permitted.

Administration of the estate of John Parke Custis was a matter that demanded consideration and action. With Mrs. Washington's approval he wrote to her brother, Bartholomew Dandridge, asking that he assume the responsibility of administrator. Washington was certain that Lund would give all the assistance in his power. If—for purposes of administration and division of property—it were necessary to have a guardian appointed for the children, he hoped that Dandrige would assume this trust.

Compelling as these matters were, there were others of even greater import. Orders must be dispatched to distant commanders. Highly congratulatory letters and resolutions, inspired by the recent victory, must be acknowledged. His capable aides, familiar with his literary style and privy to his intentions, could draft routine letters, but there were many that he must pen or dictate himself. Only he could reply to the inhabitants of Alexandria with the assurance that a peaceful return to the agreeable society of his fellow citizens was among his most ardent wishes. There must be polite expressions of appreciation to all these friendly correspondents, but he was not the same colonial-colonel-turned-general who had been so gratified by praise and honors when General Gage evacuated Boston in the spring of 1776. His enlarged outlook is revealed in a statement to a fellow officer, Gen. John Armstrong, 26 March 1781, "We ought not to look back, unless it is to derive useful lessons from past errors, and for the purpose of profiting by dear bought experience." Only he could say to a friend and well-wisher that the victory at Yorktown might better not have happened if it induced a sense of relaxation and supineness, of false security. This was the tenor of his responses to congratulatory messages from individuals and public bodies as he wrote acknowledgments from Mount Vernon and later from Philadelphia, urging preparations for another campaign. To Lafayette, as the latter sailed for France, he stressed the importance of continued naval superiority on the American coast if the war was to be brought to a speedy and successful conclusion.

On 20 December the general set out for Philadelphia, accompanied by Mrs. Washington. There he acknowledged General Rochambeau's letter of 23 December. The French general had written, "I learnt by common report that your Excellency's seat has suffered by fire." In his reply, 8 January 1782, Washington wrote, "My loss at Mount Vernon was not very considerable, but I was in the greatest danger of having my House and all the adjacent Buildings consumed." His let-

THE MOUNT VERNON STABLE

Fig. 27. This brick stable replaced the frame structure destroyed by fire in 1781. Its design was a subject of correspondence between the general in Philadelphia and his manager at Mount Vernon.

In 1785 a young English guest wrote, "I afterwards went into his stables, where among an amazing number of horses I saw old 'Nelson,' now twenty-two years of age, that carried the General almost always during the war. 'Blueskin,' another fine old horse next to him, now and then had that honor. They have heard the roaring of many a cannon in their time. 'Blueskin' was not the favorite, on account of his not standing fire so well as venerable old 'Nelson.' The General makes no manner of use of them now; he keeps them in a nice stable, where they feed away at their ease for their past services."

(Courtesy of the Mount Vernon Ladies' Association.)

ter of the same date to Lund reveals that the stable, a frame structure, had been destroyed. As the news of this event would scarcely have reached Williamsburg in three days and George Washington's brief comment does not indicate otherwise, we assume that the fire occurred before he left Mount Vernon. In the emergency his presence could have been decisive in preventing the greater loss which threatened.

Although under pressure of much other correspondence, Washington acknowledged and approved Lund's proposal for a larger stable (fig. 27). With his accustomed attention to such matters, he directed that the coach compartment should be in the middle of the structure, with a door in the pediment above for the reception of hay. He asked for dimensions that would enable him to make a plan incorporating other features of the new stable. Lund's comments were invited. Evans, the carpenter, should be consulted; the working up of rafters and joists could be set about immediately. The commander-in-chief was in daily attendance upon the Continental Congress and its committees; dispatch riders hurried to and fro seeking and carrying his orders and the most respectable inhabitants of the city sought to pay him homage, but he would find the time to draw a plan for his new Mount Vernon stable.

Peace At Last

On 23 March 1782, after a final audience with the Continental Congress, the commander-in-chief set out with Mrs. Washington to rejoin the army. Spring was in the air, and it was time to begin preparations for another campaign. Hopeful rumors of peace were also in the air, and the states had assumed the attitude of supine relaxation against which the general had warned. In early March the House of Commons passed a resolution branding as enemies of king and country all who should advise or attempt further prosecution of the war in North America. Peace seemed to be assured, but news traveled slowly and diplomatic formalities moved at an even slower pace; provisional articles were not signed in Paris until late November 1782. Meantime, General Washington, deeply distrustful of British motives and uncertain of effective French support, continued to urge a state of readiness. On 4 May, in a circular letter to the states, he wrote, "No Nation has ever yet suffered in Treaty, by preparing, even in the Moment of Negotiation, most vigorously for the field."

The army was restless. There was widespread fear among the troops that they would be mustered out with their claims of back pay unsettled, to straggle home, hungry and penniless. On 22 May the commander received a seven-page unsigned memorandum from Col. Lewis Nicola. Citing the plight of the army and the weakness of the Congress, Nicola urged a stronger form of government, in reality a monarchy. His approach was subtle, but his meaning was clear; George Washington, perhaps "under some title apparently more moderate," should become king. General Washington's response was prompt and devastating. "If I am not deceived in the knowledge of myself, you could not have found a person to whom your schemes are more disagreeable. . . . Let me conjure you then, if you have any regard for your Country, concern for yourself, or respect for me, to banish these thoughts from your Mind, and never communicate, as from yourself, or anyone else, a sentiment of the like Nature."

Mrs. Washington set out from the general's quarters at Newburgh on 10 July, en route to Mount Vernon. There would be no need on this journey to linger in Philadelphia, no fear that advancing British troops would stand in her way or lay waste her home while she was on the road. As she moved southward, a friendly French army was approaching Mount Vernon from the direction of Williamsburg; Rochambeau and his troops were moving to join the Continental army on the Hudson. The main column moved slowly, marching by night and resting by day, to avoid the extreme heat of a Tidewater Virginia summer. The officers had leisure for social amenities along the way. In Fredericksburg they paid their respects to General Washington's mother and to his sister, Mrs. Lewis. Mount Vernon was visited also, and one of its guests, Ludwig, Baron von Closen, aide to General Rochambeau, has left an account of his meeting with Mrs. Washington and his entertainment at Mount Vernon:

On the 17th we reached Colchester, on the 18th Alexandria, where I left my regiment, in view of visiting Mount Vernon, the domain of General Washington. I arrived there at nine o'clock in the morning, and was very kindly received by Administrator Lund, a kinsman of the General. I was impressed with Mr. Lund as being a worthy, unselfish man, and as well as his wife, sincerely devoted to the General, so that the latter could not have wished a better representative.

The spacious and well-contrived mansion-house at Mount Vernon was elegantly furnished, though there was no remarkable luxury to be seen anywhere; and, indeed, any ostentatious pomp would not have agreed with the simple manner of the owner. Two pavilions and a number of farm buildings completed the impression of a stately domain. A stable was just being rebuilt that had been burned down a short time before, in which accident the General had lost ten of the best of his horses. Behind the pavilion at the right there was a far-extending garden, which was kept with equal taste, and produced some of the finest fruits in the country.

The next morning I left Mount Vernon, and Mr. Lund had the kindness to accompany me as far as Alexandria. There we breakfasted at Colonel Fitzpatrick's and then proceeded toward Ebbington, the residence of Mrs. Custis. We had got about four miles on our way when we met her. She was going to Mr. Fitzgerald's, from where we were just coming. She intended to go from there by ship down the Potomac to meet her mother at the estate of Mr. Diggs, seven miles from Mr. Fitzgerald's house, on the left shore of the river. She invited us to take part in this excursion, and I did not hesitate for a moment in answering "Yes."

I thereupon returned to Alexandria and sent my horses back to Mount Vernon by land. At ten o'clock I embarked with Mrs. Custis, her friend, Miss Allens, Mr. Lund, and an intelligent young lawyer whose name I do not remember, in a pretty small boat. The town of Alexandria, lying close on the right shore of the Potomac, affords, a few miles lower down the river, an aspect of great charm. The beauties of the view were combined with merry conversation, in which the ladies set us the best example, so that time seemed to be flying away. At noon we reached the home of the family Diggs, where we were received in a most friendly manner.

Shortly after, also, Mrs. Washington arrived there, on her way home from the North River. She was accompanied by a nephew of the General's, a young man of captivating though rather sickly looking appearance. He had been suffering for some time from a slow fever, which I was told is frequently met with in Virginia.

After dinner we embarked with Mrs. Washington and her nephew in the same boat that had brought us here, in order to continue our trip to Mount Vernon, six miles down the river. On our arrival there, Mrs. Washington requested me to invite Count de Custine, who was at that moment at Colchester, with all the officers of his regiment, to dinner for the next day. The Count accepted the invitation with ten officers of the regiment, and sent Mr. Bellegarde before him with a very valuable present, a set of china, coming from his own manufactory at Niederwieler, near Pflasburg, in Lorraine. It was ornamented with the coat-of-arms and initials of General Washington, surrounded with a laurel wreath, and was received by Mrs. Washington with most hearty thanks. These gentlemen returned in the evening to Colchester, while I, for my part, remained the following day at Mount Vernon, and was then obliged to take leave, though very unwillingly. The hours I spent in Mount Vernon rank among the most delightful reminiscenses of my life.

The Mrs. Custis of von Closen's journal was, of course, Mrs. Washington's recently widowed daughter-in-law, a young woman of great vivacity and charm. The home of the family Digges was Warburton, on the Maryland shore of the Potomac a short distance above Mount Vernon. The Washingtons frequently ferried to or from Warburton when traveling between Mount Vernon and northerly destinations. The young nephew of attractive but sickly appearance was George Augustine Washington, son of the general's brother, Charles. George Augustine had a distinguished record as a dragoon in Lee's Partisan Rangers and in the Virginia campaign of the previous summer as an aide to General Lafayette. He married Mrs. Washington's niece, Fanny Bassett, in 1785 and succeeded Lund Washington as manager of Mount Ver-

A PIECE OF THE CUSTINE CHINA

Fig. 28. This little covered milk jug is a part of the set of china that the count de Custine presented to Mrs. Washington at Mount Vernon in the summer of 1782. The jug is authenticated as having been given by Mrs. Washington to Dolley Madison. It was purchased by the association in 1941. By purchase, loan, or gift, more than a dozen pieces of this service have found their way back to Mount Vernon since the association took possession in 1859. Each piece bears the initials of the general, but von Closen was in error in stating that they bear his coat of arms as well. *(Courtesy of the Mount Vernon Ladies' Association.)*

non a year later. His malady was tuberculosis; he died during his uncle's first term as president.

The china that the count de Custine presented to Mrs. Washington (see fig. 28) was politely acknowledged by General Washington in a note from headquarters the following month. In reply the Count wrote: "I have the honor to assure Your Excellency of the extreme pleasure that I experienced at Mrs. W.—accepting, with that goodness which is natural to her, the production of my Country. Your Excellency will do me but Justice in regarding this as a small testimony of my Esteem, too happy if, when I am returned to Europe, it will mean to your remembrance, one who is the most sincere admirer of these Virtues which have given Liberty to this Continent."

In the autumn of 1782, despairing of being free to lay aside his military duties and to spend some time at home, the general invited Mrs. Washington to join him at headquarters once again. She left Mount Vernon on 20 November and arrived at Newburgh on the thirtieth. The French army had marched on northward and was about to embark at Boston. Rochambeau and his staff chose a more southerly point of departure, sailing for France from Annapolis in early January 1783. These congenial companions-in-arms were very much missed; one of them, Chastellux, was numbered among General Washington's few intimates. "Without amusements or avocations," he wrote to General Heath in early February, "I am spending another Winter (I hope it will be the last I am kept from returning to domestic life) amongst these rugged and dreary Mountains." On the same day he noted in a letter to Bryan Fairfax, "At present we are fast locked in Frost and Snow; without a title of news. We look wistfully to the East, and to the South for an Arrival; supposing the first European vessel will bring the speech of the British King, the Addresses and debates there upon; the last of which I expect, will discover the Ultimatum of the National determination respecting the continuance of the War, or acceptance of Peace upon such terms as the negotiations for it have been able to strike out." In mid-January he had thanked General Knox for a sleigh, which he noted was "handsome, convenient and well executed." Knox was requested to give the workmen a couple of guineas, "to be laid out in liquor."

The commander-in-chief was increasingly concerned about the discontent of the Continental army. Congress's request to the states for authority to raise money to pay the troops by taxing imports had been denied. In mid-January the general had written satirically to brother John Augustine: "The army as usual is without pay and a great part of the soldiery without shirts; and the patience of them is equally threadbear, it seems to be a matter of small consequence to those at a distance. In truth if one were to *hazard an opinion* for them on this subject, it would be, that the army having contracted a habit of living without money, it would be injurious to it to introduce other customs." In early March, writing to his old friend Benjamin Harrison, now governor of Virginia, he predicted that if the powers of Congress were not enlarged, "anarchy and confusion must prevail."

On 19 March, in a letter to Lund, the general explained his failure to write by the earlier post:

I was too much engaged at the time, in counteracting a most insidious attempt to disturb the repose of the army, and sow the seeds of discord between the civil and military powers of the continent, to attend to small matters. The author of this attempt, whoever he may be, is yet behind the curtain; and as conjectures might be wrong, I shall be silent at present. The good sense, the virtue, and patient forbearance of the army, on this, as upon every other trying occasion which has happened to call them into action, has again triumphed: and appear'd with more lustre than ever.

If the states did not enable the congress to meet its obligations, he wrote, he would not predict the consequences.

In this letter to Lund and in his official correspondence, Washington omits mention of his confrontation with the officers of the army at a meeting that he had called on 15 March. His audience had been resentful and angry, but respectful, well aware that he was their advocate and that he himself had served without pay for nearly eight years. One of his aides, Colonel Cobb, wrote that as he took the podium, Washington said, "Gentlemen, you will permit me to put on my spectacles, for I have not only grown gray, but almost blind, in the service of my country." This simple statement was more effective than his formal plea for moderation and his promise of a continued effort for redress of their grievances. The possibility of an armed confrontation with the civil authorities was forestalled. In *Washington, the Indispensable Man*, James Flexner says that this meeting was "probably the most important single gathering ever held in the United States." He quotes a comment by Thomas Jefferson, "The moderation and virtue of a single character probably prevented this Revolution from being closed, as most others have been, by a subversion of that liberty it was intended to establish."

On 12 March 1783, a vessel arrived in Philadelphia, bringing the official text of a preliminary treaty that had been signed in Paris on 20 January. On 15 April the treaty was ratified by Congress. On the eighteenth the commander-in-chief ordered a cessation of hostilities, which was to be publicly proclaimed at headquarters the following day, the eighth anniversary of the battle of Lexington and Concord. An extra ration of liquor was to be issued in order that all might drink to "perpetual Peace, Independence and Happiness to the United States of America."

To Tench Tilgham, his former aide who had returned to civilian life, Washington wrote: "No Man, indeed, can relish the approaching Peace with more heartfelt, and grateful satisfaction than myself. A Mind always upon the stretch, and tortured with a diversity of perplexing circumstances, needed a respite, and I anticipate the pleasure of a little repose and retirement." He was, he wrote, still encompassed with difficulties and each day brought fresh sources of uneasiness. In this letter he graciously acknowledged his indebtedness to the select group of aides who had shared his trouble and lightened his burdens, adding, "to none of these can I ascribe a greater share of merit than to you." Writing to his longtime friend Governor Benjamin Harrison of Virginia, he referred once

again to "that relaxation and repose which is absolutely necessary to me." He was war weary and homesick; eight years
of service without leave, of unremitting responsibility under
the most trying circumstances, had taken their toll. He had
aged, most visibly to those about him, in the last three years.
His teeth were increasingly troublesome. Since early man-
hood he had had dental problems. During the war there had
been little relief from aching teeth and the discomfort of
faulty dentures. Now, with the declaration of a preliminary
peace, one of his aides, Col. William Smith, had been allowed
to enter New York. In May the general requested the colonel
to check the credentials of a French dentist, Le Mayeur, who
had been permitted by the British to establish a practice in
the city. As Le Mayeur came to headquarters and his professional services to his distinguished patient extended thereafter
over a period of years, bringing him to Mount Vernon on a
number of occasions, it may be assumed that he was more
than ordinarily competent.

In his letters to Tilghman and Governor Harrison, Washington urged that Congress must have powers competent to
the general purposes of government, otherwise, "we may well
be compared to a rope of Sand." Unreasonable jealousy and
ill-founded prejudices must not be allowed to destroy "the
goodly fabrick we have been Eight years laboring to erect."
Passages of the same import appear in his letters of this period
to other close friends, in Virginia and elsewhere—to Arthur
Lee, Theodorick Bland, his brother John Augustine, Alexander Hamilton, Nathanael Greene, Elias Boudinot, and Lafayette. Hamilton's thoughts were solicited.

In June 1783, Washington issued his "Circular to the
States" in the form of a letter to the governor of each state
with a request that they communicate his sentiments to their
respective legislatures. It is a document of over four thousand
words, inspired by his own "dear bought experience" of the
past eight years and the hope that his fellow citizens might
derive useful lessons therefrom. There are four things that he
feels are essential to the well-being—to the very existence, in
fact—of the United States as an independent power. Three

of these—a sacred regard for public justice, the adoption of a proper peacetime military establishment, and a pacific and friendly disposition among the people of the United States—are scarcely controversial. The fourth (actually the first in his order of listing), an indissoluble union under one federal head, might appear to be a commendable objective also, yet the timing and the urgent tone of the writer's plea is an evidence of his fear that thirteen loosely federated sovereign states in this period of political probation might further relax the ties that bound them, with disastrous results.

This circular letter to the states came to be known as "Washington's Legacy." There can be no doubt that he intended it to be a final testament, a declaration of his hope and faith, his vision of a new nation. He wrote of a retirement "in which I meditate to pass the remainder of life in undisturbed repose." He gave his "final blessing to the Country" and reiterated "the determination I have formed, of not taking any share in public business hereafter." Surely, as the military leader of the Revolution he had done his part. He would return to his rural pursuits at Mount Vernon, leaving the responsibility of a peaceful political evolution to the elected legislatures of the states and the delegates in the Continental Congress. For the moment at least his misgivings would be muted by his belief in the Providence that had brought the war to a successful conclusion. The letter closes with a pious benediction:

I now make it my earnest prayer, that God would have you, and the State over which you preside, in his holy protection, that he would incline the hearts of the Citizens to cultivate a spirit of subordination and obedience to Government, to entertain a brotherly affection and love for one another, for their fellow Citizens of the United States at large, and particularly for their brethren who have served in the Field, and finally, that he would most graciously be pleased to dispose us all, to do Justice, to love mercy, and to demean ourselves with that Charity, humility and pacific temper of mind, which were the Characteristicks of the Divine Author of our blessed Religion, and without an humble imitation of whose example in these things, we can never hope to be a happy Nation.

The reception of this letter was in most instances favorable. The responses of the governors were eulogistic in tone; the legislatures passed complimentary resolves. But in the Virginia legislature, Fitzpatrick notes, there were murmurs "against what is called the unsolicited obtrusion of his advice." There were other and more local voices of dissent also. In an address of 30 May 1783 from his own neighbors, "Fairfax County Freeholders," to their delegates in the legislature, there was evidence of a looming political struggle. Circumstantially—and, in the opinion of the editor of his papers, Robert A. Rutland, with overwhelming evidence to support that conclusion—this document is attributed to Washington's longtime friend and ally George Mason of Gunston Hall. The address asserts that "the separate States only can safely have the power of levying taxes." It recommends that Virginia's delegates to the Congress be instructed to oppose the sending of ambassadors to the courts of Europe. Opposition is urged to all encroachments of the American Congress on the sovereignty and jurisdiction of the separate states. The retiring general's determination to take no part in public affairs would be severely tested by the menace of such sentiments. That "absolutely necessary" repose and relaxation might prove to be but a mirage if what he believed to be the fairest opportunity for political happiness with which a people had ever been favored were to be jeopardized by such sentiments as those espoused by his provincial neighbors.

General Washington's patience was severely taxed by the long period of waiting for final ratification of the peace treaty. His private affairs had suffered inevitably by reason of his long-enforced absence from home. He was increasingly anxious to return and to take the reins of management once again into his own hands. His surviving letters to Lund Washington during this interval reflect a desire for exact information about harvests and the state of his finances. Lund had not submitted a statement of receipts and expenses since the spring of 1778, when he had visited Valley Forge. He was frank in confessing his delinquency. Of an overdue statement he wrote, in January 1783, that he still intended to send it, "but so it is that I generally put off writing from one day to another. I had rather be employed in the most laborious way than copying any writing whatever and this it is that makes me often neglect a work of that kind and causes me often to keep irregular accounts. Not from ignorance, but neglect. At present I believe I shall send it by the next post."

This procrastination provoked a stern reprimand and an unequivocal demand for an accounting. "I want to know," the General wrote, "before I come home (as I shall come home with empty pockets whenever Peace shall take place) how affairs stand with me and what my dependence is." He was annoyed by Lund's failure to collect rents from tenants in four Viginia counties to the west of Mount Vernon. In eight years Lund had made but one round of these detached holdings, and that not complete. On that occasion he had collected but twenty pounds from the delinquent tenants. Spurred by his employer's criticism of his "unconquerable aversion to going from home," he set forth once again, and on his return he reported that he had been able to collect nothing but a few promises of future payment. Worst of all, Lund had failed to draw his own wages since April of 1778, and his belated accounting showed a cash balance unequal to the amount due him. "I shall be more hurt than at anything else," the general wrote, "to think that an Estate which I have drawn nothing from for eight years, and which always enabled me to make any purchase I had in mind, should not have been able, for the last five years to pay the manager and that, worse than going home to empty coffers, and expensive living, I shall be encumbered with debt. It is disagreeable to me, because I dare say it will be so to you, to make these observations; but as my public business is now drawing to a close, I cannot avoid looking to my private concerns, which do not wear the most smiling countenance."

The spirit of this passage seems ungenerous. If Lund's wages were the only indebtedness chargeable to the estate under his management, it would have been handsomely overbalanced by the structural improvements which had been made during the war. There may have been other extenuat-

ing circumstances. Lund's poor bookkeeping and a mutilation
of his ledger obscure the record. It was his misfortune to be
judged by the same high standard that his employer set for
himself. Fortunately for their relationship, judgment was
tempered by the realization on the general's part that Lund's
solid virtues outweighed his faults, and these occasional verbal chastisements seem never to have impaired their friendly
intimacy.

The cessation of hostilities did make possible a renewal at
Mount Vernon of building activities that had been suspended
for lack of workmen and materials. Carpenters, plasterers,
bricklayers, and painters were busy about the place. Work on
the new stable was pressed. Paint was still a scarce commodity, but enough was found in Alexandria, Yorktown, and
Philadelphia to cover the mansion and its principal dependencies. The paint purchased in Philadelphia was of poor
quality, Lund complained; some of it had been watered. In
late January 1783, he predicted that completion of the stable
would employ two carpenters all winter. Later in the year
there are notations in his account book of payments for un-
derpinning the coach house and laying up a chimney in the
washhouse. There are also entries recording payments for
plastering the interior of the washhouse and the ceilings of the
covered ways that connect the mansion and its two principal
dependencies. In August, the general was much annoyed by
a report of serious leakage in the mansion roof. The workman
at fault, he thought, must be "a miserable artisan or a very
great rascal indeed." After his return home, he found it necessary to reshingle the west side of the roof.

General Washington's return would place a time limitation
on Lund and Betsey's occupancy of the mansion and would
allow them the option of living on their own property, a tract
of land adjoining Mount Vernon on the west, a part at least
of which Lund had purchased from his employer some years
earlier. Here a homesite was chosen, and construction commenced in 1782; the house, a commodious structure of brick,
was completed in 1784. This new home, which Lund called
"Hayfield," was the realization of his ambition to own a mod-

est place where he could, as he expressed it, "live and give a neighbor beef and toddy." Here he passed the remainder of his days in peaceful retirement after leaving George Washington's service at the end of 1785.

There was little exaggeration in George Washington's statements to Lund that he was coming home with empty pockets to empty coffers. In February 1784, when a nephew, a son of his late brother-in-law Fielding Lewis, solicited a loan he wrote:

You very much mistake my circumstances when you suppose me in a condition to advance money. I made no money from my Estate during the nine years I was absent from it, and brought none home with me, those who owed me, for the most part, took advantage of the depreciation and paid me off with six pence in the pound, those to whom I was indebted, I have yet to pay, without other means, if they will not wait, than selling part of my Estate; or distressing those who were too honest to take advantage of the tender Laws to quit scores with me.

This relation of my circumstances, which is a true one, is alone sufficient (without adding that my living under the best economy I can use, must unavoidably be expensive) to convince you of my inability to advance money.

He did manage to scrape together a hundred guineas to finance a journey to the West Indies in pursuit of health for another nephew, George Augustine Washington. When his brother John Augustine asked for a loan, he was unable to accommodate him, but offered to endorse his note if he could find the money elsewhere.

During the winter and spring of 1783, General Washington found time to prepare a summary of his official expenses for submission to the Congress. This statement, in his own hand with supporting vouchers, is dated 1 July 1783. It accounts for the moneys advanced by the Congress or its agent and, on the other side of the ledger, all of the expenditures for the support of his official household and his travels and much of the expense for secret service agents, whose names and activities were protected by unidentified advances from his own military chest. Dr. Fitzpatrick, who published this account in facsimile with his own notes, reports these expenses to have totaled, from June 1775 through December 1783, £20,433–16–9. It would be difficult to equate this sum with the present dollar. By Washington's reckoning of six shillings to the dollar, it equalled $68,110. In 1933 Fitzpatrick gave it a current value of $200,000. By any table of conversion, it was a modest sum.

After some deliberation the general included in his statement of expenses a charge of £1,064–1–0 for Mrs. Washington's wartime travels between Mount Vernon and his winter quarters. At first view, he noted, this had the complexion of a private charge and he had doubts about the propriety of including it, "But the peculiar circumstances attending my command, and the embarrassed situation of our Public affairs which obliged me (to the no small detriment of my private Interest) to postpone the visit I every year contemplated to make my Family between the close of one Campaign and opening of another—and as this expence was incidental thereto, & consequent of my self denial I have, as of right I think I ought, upon due consideration adjudged the charge as just with respect to myself; . . ." In further justification of the charge he noted that he had from time to time applied his private funds to public purposes, which ". . . thro' hurry, I suppose, & the perplexity of business. . . ." he had "omitted to charge," while every debit against himself had been recorded.

A memorandum in the general's hand, which supports this charge for Mrs. Washington's travels, is in the Mount Vernon collection. Except for her final wartime journey from headquarters to Mount Vernon in October 1783 and those occasions when she traveled with her husband between headquarters and Philadelphia or other points, all of her journeys are recorded, with the charges incurred. As a testimonial of the devotion and fortitude of Martha Washington, if for no other reason, this account deserves to be included here:

An Acc^t. of M^{rs}. Washington's Expences from Virginia to my Winter Quarters & back again to Virginia according to the Mem^{ms}.

Martha Washington's Trunk

Fig. 29. A label affixed to the inner surface of the lid by Eliza Parke Custis Law identifies this as the trunk "in which the cloaths of my Sainted Grandmother Mrs. Washington were always pack'd by her own hands when she went to visit, & spend sometime with the General, whenever the Army were in quarters. I have stood by it as she put in her cloaths sadly distress'd at her going away—& oh how joyfully when she returned did I look on to see her cloaths taken out, & the many gifts she always brought for her grandchildren."
(Courtesy of the Mount Vernon Ladies' Association.)

and acc^{ts} which I have received from her & those who accomp^d. her.

		Lawful		
1775. Dec^r.	To amount of her Exp^s. from Virginia to Cambridge	‡ 85	2	6
1776. July.	To Ditto from New York to Virginia after the Enemy Landed	‡ 100	2	8

on Staten Island Including her residence in Philadelphi^a. at Board for sometime p^r. acc^t. ...

1777. Mar.}	To Ditto from Virginia to Morris Town while the Troops lay there in Wint^r. Q^{rs}.	‡	61	10	–
May.	To Ditto from Morris Town to Virg^a. including a few days Stay in Philadelp^a.	‡	74	—	
1778. Feb.}	To Ditto from Virg^a. to Valley Forge	‡	52	8	6
June.	To Ditto from Valley Forge back to Virg^a. when the army took the Field	‡	54	—	–
Dec^r.	To Ditto. to Phil^a. where I then was at the request of Congress	‡	48	—	–
1779. June.}	To Ditto back to Virginia from Middleb^k. when the army marched from its Cantonments at that place	‡	72	—	
Dec^r. {	To Ditto in coming to Morris town when the army was cantoned in the vecinity of it	‡	63	5	
1780. June.{	To Ditto on her return to Virginia from that place	‡	68	—	–
Nov. {	To Ditto—her Expences to my Quart^{rs}. at New Windsor	‡	78	6	8
June.	To Ditto back to Virginia from	‡	85	—	–

1781.{	thence, when the army took the field—Including a few days stay in Philad^a.			
July 1782.{	To her Expences from Newburgh to Virginia	‡ 72	—	–
Dec^r.	To Ditto from Virginia to New-burgh	‡ 70	5	8
		£1064	1	–

Errors Excepted

July 1st., 1783 ..... G. Washington

On 2 November 1783 the commander-in-chief issued his "Farewell Orders to the Armies of the United States" from Rocky Hill, New Jersey, where he had been quartered since early August in attendance on the Continental Congress at nearby Princeton, that timorous body having removed from Philadelphia when mutinous Pennsylvania troops disrupted its deliberations. News of the signing of the definitive treaty of peace in Paris on 3 September had been received in Princeton on 1 November. The war was over. "The curtain of separation will soon be drawn and the military scene will be closed to him forever," as Washington expressed it in the closing sentence of his farewell orders. A week later the wagons containing his baggage were directed to proceed to Mount Vernon. "As you know, they contain all my papers, which are of immense value to me," he reminded the escorting officer in his letter of instruction.

Mrs. Washington had left for Mount Vernon in early October, "before the weather and roads should get bad," the General noted in his letter of 12 October to Lafayette. For the general's lady the war had ended none too soon. She had been prostrated by a fever at Newburgh and was still unwell when she left Rocky Hill. Early in the new year she wrote to a friend, Mrs. Elias Boudinot, from Mount Vernon:

It would give me infinite pleasure to see you Mr and Miss Boudenot at this place—without which I almost dispair of ever enjoy-
ing that happyness, as my frequent long Journeys have not only
left me without inclination to undertake another, but almost dis-
qualified me from doing it, as I find the fatiegue is too much for me
to bear. My little family are all with me; and have been very well
till with in these few days, that they have been taken with the
measles.—the worst I hope is over, and that I shall soon have them
prattling about me again.—with best respects to Mr Boudenot, and
love to Miss Susan and yourself—in which the General joins.

Anxious as General Washington was to follow Martha to
Mount Vernon, he could not relinquish his command or delegate responsibility while the British remained in possession of
New York. Finally, on 25 November, accompanied by Governor George Clinton and escorted by a numerous retinue of
military and political personages, the general rode into the
city, hard on the heels of the embarking British troops. He
was detained in New York until 4 December as the British
flotilla made final preparations for a wintry crossing of the
North Atlantic and awaited a favoring wind. His time was
much occupied by festivals and dinners. There were numerous congratulatory addresses to be received and acknowledged. On the fourth he said farewell to a group of his fellow
officers at Fraunces Tavern and was rowed across the Hudson as the British fleet made sail from the lower bay. He was
bound for Annapolis to resign his commission to the Continental Congress, which had adjourned to that city from
Princeton. His command had been reduced to the three aides
who accompanied him. He would have preferred the role of
a modern Cincinnatus quietly returning to his agricultural
pursuits, but his passage was marked by constant repetitions
of the testimonials which had been accorded him in New
York. As he approached Philadelphia he was welcomed by a
numerous party and escorted to his quarters. Church bells
rang and cannon boomed as "the people testified their satisfaction at once more seeing their illustrious chief, by repeated
acclamation," according to the *Pennsylvania Packet* of 9 December. In Philadelphia, between fetes and laudatory formal-

CINCINNATI CHINA

Fig. 30. In 1785 George Washington purchased, through his friend Col. Henry Lee ("Light-Horse Harry") a set of Nanking china that had just arrived in New York from the Orient. The service numbered 302 pieces. It bears the insignia of the Society of the Cincinnati, of which Washington was the first president general. The little tureen here illustrated is one of fifteen pieces of this service in the Mount Vernon collection.
(Courtesy of the Mount Vernon Ladies' Association.)

ities, the general found time to do some Christmas shopping. For Mrs. Washington he bought a locket and a dress cap; for his three little stepgranddaughters, small pocketbooks, thimbles, sashes, and children's books; for the stepgrandson, his namesake, age two and a half, a whirligig, a small fiddle, and a toy gun. He also purchased a handsome silver coffeepot with his coat of arms engraved.

On Friday, 19 December, the general arrived in Annapolis for the last scenes in his dramatic progression. Of the three aides who had left New York with him, Humphreys and

GEORGE WASHINGTON'S BOOKPLATE

Fig. 31. "Exitus acta probat." This sentence appears in Ovid's *Heroides* and in that context has been translated "the event proves well the wisdom of her course." A standard dictionary of foreign terms offers two translations: "the issue proves (or justifies) the deeds; all's well that ends well." Lenin's disciples might prefer "the end justifies the means." Perhaps we should accept the version submitted by a member of the language department of George Washington University, "the outcome tests the deeds," or the scriptural admonition, "by their deeds ye shall know them." *(Courtesy of the Mount Vernon Ladies' Association.)*

A HANDSOME ADDITION TO THE FAMILY SILVER

Fig. 32. This coffeepot was purchased by General Washington from Joseph Anthony, silversmith, when he stopped in Philadelphia en route to a Christmas homecoming at Mount Vernon in December 1783. The coat of arms was a heritage from the general's English ancestors. Many pieces of the Mount Vernon flat silver bear this griffin crest. Fragments of crest or the full coat of arms survive in the impressed wax with which the general sealed his letters.
(Courtesy of the Mount Vernon Ladies' Association.)

Walker were still in attendance. Congress, which was trying to rally a quorum for the occasion, elected to receive him on the following Tuesday.

The delay was not unwelcome. For George Washington Annapolis was a place of many happy associations. It was the center of the political and social life of Maryland, the counterpart of Virginia's prewar Williamsburg, with the advantage of being two days nearer to Mount Vernon in travel time than was Virginia's capital. Here in the years before the war the Virginia colonel had lodged with the colonial governor, Sir Robert Eden, who like himself was a keen judge of horses and a patron of the track. Together they had attended the races, dined with the Jockey Club, and attended the theater. There were faces missing now, but there were still many well-remembered Marylanders about, many callers to be received—and their calls returned. There were addresses, from the governor and the Council of Maryland, from the General Assembly, from the mayor and council of the city. To the latter he acknowledged his indebtedness for the greatest of earthly rewards, "the approbation and affections of a free people."

On Monday the Congress gave him a public dinner. In the manner of the times, there were many toasts. His own was prophetic—"Competent powers to Congress for general purposes." That evening the governor gave a ball at the state house that was attended by a numerous and brilliant company. The general, it was reported, "danced every set that all the ladies might have the pleasure of dancing with him or, as it has since been handsomely expressed, 'get a touch of him.'"

Promptly at twelve o'clock the next day, the general, flanked by his two aides, presented himself at the state house and entered the chamber where the Congress awaited him, seated and with their hats on. Humphreys had made a fair copy of his address for reading and submission to the Congress, but it was his own composition. The document is equally notable for its contents and its omissions. He resigns "with satisfaction" the appointment he had accepted "with diffidence." He acknowledges his overall obligation to the army and more particularly to the officers who composed his official family. "The patronage of Heaven" is given due recognition. In his retained draft the writer bade a "final farewell" to Congress and took "ultimate leave" of public life. But he struck out the word "final" and ran a line through "ultimate"; they do not appear in Humphreys's fair copy. In the last sentence of this three-minute address, there appears the inevitable figure of speech, "I retire from the great theatre of action."

The brief ceremony was soon over. The general handed his commission and the copy of his address to the president of Congress. The pressing throng of spectators was dismissed, Congress formally adjourned, the newly translated private citizen shook the hand of each delegate and said goodbye. The door of the state house closed behind him and the great dome of the structure faded rapidly into the background as he and his aides rode off at a good pace toward Mount Vernon, where he had an engagement to dine on Christmas Day with Mrs. Washington. There is no record of this final leg of his homeward journey. He kept no diary for the years 1782 and 1783, nor is there a cash memorandum to identify the Maryland tavern that was patronized on the night of the twenty-third, no record of a ferry toll to tell us where the party crossed the Potomac. A letter to Lafayette from Mount Vernon weeks later confirms that he reached home in time to keep his engagement, "at Anapolis where Congress were then and are now sitting, I did on the 23rd of December present them my commission, and made them my last bow and on the Eve of Christmas entered these doors, an older man by near nine years, than when I left them."

In this letter to Lafayette (1 February 1784) the master of Mount Vernon also confirmed his renunciation of the busy scenes of public life and his determination to rusticate "under the shadow of my own vine and fig tree." He was fifty-two, still vigorous, but he was already oppressed by premonitions of his own mortality. The Washingtons were short-lived: his great-grandfather, John the Emigrant, had died at the age of forty-six; his grandfather Lawrence in his thirty-eighth year;

THE PINE PORTRAITS

Fig. 33. On 28 April 1785, the general noted in his diary that Robert Edge Pine, "a pretty eminent Portrait and Historical Painter," had arrived "in order to take my picture from the life." Pine came bearing letters of introduction from George William Fairfax, Robert Morris, and others. The artist was three weeks at Mount Vernon. His subjects, in addition to the general, were Mrs. Washington's four grandchildren and her niece, Fanny Bassett. Fanny was about to marry the general's nephew, George Augustine Washington, and the record indicated that Pine's portrait of her was a wedding present to the young couple. In a letter to a friend, the general's secretary, Tobias Lear, described Fanny as "one of those superior beings who are sent down to bless good men." Her portrait was placed in the west parlor of the mansion. The portraits of the four grandchildren hung in General and Mrs. Washington's bedchamber.
Fig. 33a. Fanny Bassett Washington (1767–96)
(Courtesy of the Mount Vernon Ladies' Association.)

his father had died at the age of forty-nine; his younger brother, Samuel, was only forty-seven at the time of his death early in 1782. Of the two elder half brothers, Lawrence had died at thirty-four and Austin at forty-two. For him time could well be running out and he was determined, he assured Lafayette, "to be pleased with all; and this my dear friend being the order of my life, I will move gently down the stream of life, until I sleep with my Fathers."

Fig. 33b. Eliza Parke Custis (1776–1832)
(From the Collection of Washington and Lee University, Lexington, Virginia.)

Fig. 33c. Martha Parke Custis (1777–1854)
(Courtesy of the Mount Vernon Ladies' Association.)

Fig. 33d. Eleanor Parke Custis (1779–1852)
(Courtesy of the Mount Vernon Ladies' Association.)

Fig. 33e. George Washington Parke Custis (1781–1857)
(From the Collection of Washington and Lee University, Lexington, Virginia.)

There is a remarkable parallel between the Mount Vernon domestic scene at this happy holiday season in 1783 and the scene here twenty-four years earlier, when George and Martha Washington spent their first Christmas together in their own home. Then as now there had been two young children, a boy and a girl. Then also George Washington had just completed a military career, one that marked him as Virginia's most distinguished soldier. At that time, too, he had believed that he was retiring from public life. To his distant cousin and London agent, Richard Washington, he had written on 20 September 1759, "I am now I believe fixd at this Seat with an agreable Consort for Life and hope to find more happiness in retirement than I ever experienced amidst a wide and bustling World." Sixteen uninterrupted years together had been granted them before that day in the spring of 1775 when the Virginia colonel set out for Philadelphia. Had his hope of happiness with an agreeable consort been realized? There is strong affirmation in his letter of 18 June 1775, to "My Dearest," reporting his new military command, "I should enjoy more real happiness in one month with you at home, than I have the most distant prospect of finding abroad, if my stay were to be seven times seven years." There is affirmation in the invitations to Mrs. Washington to join him each autumn at headquarters. Had there been something less than strong mutual devotion and need of one another, those strenuous and precarious journeys to the general's winter quarters might never have been made.

There is affirming testimony also in the general's letters to two French correspondents. Only a man happily adjusted to the state of matrimony could have written to a former comrade-in-arms, Charles Armand-Tuffin, the marquis de la Rouerie (10 August 1786), "For in my estimation more permanent and genuine happiness is to be found in the sequestered walks of connubial life, than in the giddy rounds of promiscuous pleasure, or the more tumultuous and imposing scenes of successful ambition. This sentiment will account, in a degree, for my not making a visit to Europe." In April 1788 he wrote to the marquis de Chastellux on the occasion of his

HOUDON'S BUST OF WASHINGTON

Fig. 34. Houdon's original bust of George Washington, modeled in clay and left at Mount Vernon by the artist, 1785.

(Courtesy of the Mount Vernon Ladies' Association.)

marriage, "Now you are well served for coming to fight in favor of the American rebels, all the way across the Atlantic Ocean, by catching that terrible Contagion, domestic felicity, which like the small pox or the plague, a man can have only once in his life; because it commonly lasts him (at least with us in America, I dont know how you manage these matters in France) for his whole life time."

At the moment of reunion this Christmas Eve of 1783, sixteen years of domestic felicity remained to George and Martha Washington. Only half of this period would be spent at Mount Vernon, but there or at the seat of the new government they would be constantly together in a congenial family setting, surrounded by Mrs. Washington's grandchildren and by nieces and nephews from both sides of the family—Custises, Washingtons, Lewises, Dandridges, and Bassetts. The sequestered life that the citizen-soldier had envisioned would prove to have been a mirage, as "a kind of destiny" drew him once again to assume the leading role on the stage of public life, but in the domestic sphere, at least, his days would be serene and happy.

Simple Truth is his best his Greatest Eulogy.

She alone can render his Fame immortal.

Abigail Adams, January 1800

Selected Bibliography

Index

Selected Bibliography

Adams, Abigail. *New Letters of Abigail Adams 1788–1801.* Edited by Stewart Mitchell. Boston: Houghton Mifflin Co., 1947.

Baker, William S. *Itinerary of General Washington from June 15, 1775, to December 23, 1783.* Philadelphia: J. B. Lippincott Co., 1892.

Bezanson, Anne, et al. *Prices and Inflation during the American Revolution, Pennsylvania, 1770–1790.* Philadelphia: University of Pennsylvania Press, 1951.

Bonsal, Stephen. *When the French Were Here; a Narrative of the Sojourn of the French Forces in America, and Their Contribution to the Yorktown Campaign, Drawn from Unpublished Reports and Letters of Participants in the National Archives of France, Ms Divison of the Library of Congress.* New York: Doubleday, Doran & Co., 1945.

Carter, Landon. *The Diary of Colonel Landon Carter of Sabine Hall, 1752–1778.* Edited by Jack P. Greene. 2 vols. Charlottesville: The University Press of Virginia, 1965.

Chastellux, Francois de Beauvoir, Marquis de. *Travels in North America in the Years 1780, 1781, and 1782.* Edited by Howard C. Rice, Jr. 2 vols. Chapel Hill: University of North Carolina Press, 1963.

Cresswell, Nicholas. *The Journal of Nicholas Cresswell, 1774–1777.* Edited by Lincoln MacVeagh. New York: Dial Press, 1924.

Custis, George Washington Parke. *Recollections and Private*

Memoirs of Washington by his adopted son, George Washington Parke Custis, With a Memoir of the author by his daughter; and Illustrative and Explanatory Notes by Benson J. Lossing. New York: Derby & Jackson, 1860.

Fithian, Philip Vickers. *Journal and Letters of Philip Vickers Fithian, 1773–74.* Williamsburg, Va.: Colonial Williamsburg, Inc., 1943.

Fitzpatrick, John C. *George Washington Himself.* Indianapolis: The Bobbs-Merrill Company, 1933.

Flexner, James Thomas. *Washington, the Indispensable Man.* Boston and Toronto: Little, Brown & Co., 1974.

Freeman, Douglas Southall. *George Washington: A Biography.* 7 vols. New York: Charles Scribner's Sons, 1948–57.

Goodrich, Charles A. *History of the United States of America.* Hartford, Conn.: D. F. Robinson & Co., 1830.

Goodwin, Rutherfoord. *A Brief & True Report Concerning Williamsburg in Virginia.* Williamsburg, Va.: Colonial Williamsburg, Inc., 1940.

Hamilton, Stanislaus, ed. *Letters to George Washington.* 5 vols. Boston and New York: Houghton Mifflin, 1898–1902.

Hendrick, Burton J. *The Lees of Virginia.* New York: Halcyon House, 1935.

Honyman, Robert. "News of the Yorktown Campaign: The Journal of Dr. Robert Honyman, April 17–November 25, 1781." Edited by Richard K. MacMaster. *The Virginia Magazine of History and Biography.* 79, no. 4 (October 1971):387–426.

Lee, Richard Henry. *The Letters of Richard Henry Lee.* Edited by James C. Ballagh. 2 vols. Macmillan Co. New York, 1911–14.

Lossing, Benson J. *Mount Vernon and its Associations.* New York, 1859.

Madison, James. *A Biography in His Own Words.* Edited by Merrill D. Peterson. New York: Newsweek and Harper & Row, Publishers, 1974.

Mason, George. *The Papers of George Mason, 1725–1792.* 3 vols. Chapel Hill: University of North Carolina Press, 1970.

Miller, Helen Hill. *George Mason: Gentleman Revolutionary.* Chapel Hill: University of North Carolina Press, 1975.

Rowland, Kate Mason. *The Life of George Mason.* New York: Putnam, 1892.

Rutland, Robert A. *George Mason, Reluctant Statesman.* Charlottesville: Dominion Books, The University Press of Virginia, 1963.

Selby, John E. A Chronology of Virginia and the War of Independence, 1763–1783. Charlottesville: published for the Virginia Independence Bicentennial Commission by the University Press of Virginia, 1973.

Thane, Elswyth. *Potomac Squire.* New York: Duell, Sloan and Pearce, 1963.

Tilghman, Oswald. *Memoir of Lieut. Col. Tench Tilghman.* . . . Albany: J. Muncell, 1876. Reprint edition, New York: Arno Press, 1971.

Torbert, Alice Coyle. *Eleanor Calvert and Her Circle.* New York: The Williams-Frederick Press, 1950.

Van Doren, Carl. *Benjamin Franklin.* New York: Viking Press, 1938.

Ward, Christopher. *The War of the Revolution.* Edited by John Richard Alden. 2 vols. New York: The Macmillan Company, 1952.

Washington, George. *Accounts of Expenses while Commander in Chief of the Continental Army, 1775–1783: Reproduced in Fascimile.* Edited by John C. Fitzpatrick. Boston and New York: Houghton Mifflin Co., 1917.

———. *The Diaries of George Washington.* Vols. 1–4, 1748–86. Edited by Donald Jackson; Dorothy Twohig, associate editor. Charlottesville: The University Press of Virginia, 1976–78.

———. *The Writings of George Washington from the Original Manuscript Sources, 1745–1799.* Edited by John C. Fitzpatrick. 39 vols. Washington, D.C.: U.S. Government Printing Office, 1931–44.

Index

In this index, MV = Mount Vernon, MW = Martha Washington, and GW = George Washington. Italicized page numbers indicate pages on which illustrations appear.